T0328350

Of Bushmen and Work

Models, Modelling and Illusions

Inaugural Lecture

Of Bushmen and Work
Models, Modelling and Illusions

Inaugural Lecture

by

Dafe Otobo

malthouse 𝜆𝒫

Malthouse Press Limited

Lagos, Benin, Ibadan, Jos,Port-Harcourt, Zaria

Malthouse Press Limited
43 Onitana Street, Off Stadium Hotel Road,
Off Western Avenue, Lagos Mainland
E-mail: malthouse_press@yahoo.com
malthouselagos@gmail.com
Website: malthouselagos.com
Tel: +234 802 600 3203

Distributors:
African Books Collective Ltd
Email: abc@africanbookscollective.com
Website: http://www.africanbookscollective.com

Acknowledgements

I am greatly indebted to my teachers at the University of Ibadan: Essien Udom, Ojetunji Aboyade, Billy Dudley, Okediji, Imoagene, Otite, Akeredolu-Ale, Onoge, Ogionwo, Soleye, Sofola and Bolaji Akinyemi. Prof. T. M. Yesufu availed me the benefit of his extensive knowledge of and comments on the Nigerian trade union scene while I was a graduate student at the London School of Economics and Political Science. I was fully exposed to intricacies of British trade unionism and state of European labour relations by my teachers at the LSE's Department of Industrial Relations: Ben Roberts, Keith Thurley, Stephen Hill, Baroness Sears, David Winchester, Jennard and Roy Lewis.

Oxford contacts include Alan Fox, Richard Hyman, Lord W. E. J. McCarthy, Vic Allen and Gavin Williams. Margery Nicholson (formerly British TUC, International Division, who was on first name terms with Nigerian trade union leaders in 1950s and 1960s) was particularly helpful in putting the TUC's policies into proper perspective. George Foggon's (OBE) reminiscences on his role and experiences as Nigeria's Permanent Secretary Commissioner for Labour (1954-1959) were invaluable and provided answers to some very awkward questions. Arthur Marsh (OBE) for his mentoring, friendship, and supervision of my doctoral thesis. Jim Lavis for his friendship and for introducing me to Malthouse UK Publishing Ltd. Robert King for his warmth and friendship; my African and Nigerian fellow students, especially Hakeem Belo-Osagie, Udoma Udo Udoma, Ike Osakwe, Stella Amachree, Sokari Braide, Chris Anyaegbunam, Evance Kalula, Jeff Modechai, Korantema Kwapong, Kwamena Akhoi, and Alero Ayida (who later became Mrs Otobo); it was fun and debates in African Society were lively.

Nigerian trade union leaders were particularly accommodating and provided invaluable information in spite of obviously, embarrassing and searching questions and my usual insistence on further clarification of sensitive issues. Lack of space compels me to mention but a few, starting with the "old brigade": Alhaji Adebola, L. Borha, Alhaji Kaltungo, V. I. M. Jack, N. F. Pepple, E.O.A. Odeyemi, Okon Eshiett, Ijeh, J. O. James and Okwese of the United Labour Congress of Nigeria (ULCN); Wahab Goodluck, S. U. Bassey, Hudson Momodu, Richard Aghedo, SOZ Ejiofoh, and Dr. Otegbeye of the Nigerian Trade, Union Congress (NTUC); and Chukwurah, Anunobi, Enigbokan, Akpan and Ramos of the Nigerian Workers Council (NWC). Special gratitude to 'Labour Leader No. 1', Michael Imoudu, for reconstructing the early years of Nigerian unionism for me in 1976. Then the other trade union leaders and bureaucrats; Comrades Joseph Akinlaja, Hassan Sunmonu, Aliyu Dangiwa, Ali Ciroma, Pascal Bayfau, Anigbo, Lasisi Osunde, Peterside, Dr Chris Imoisili, Frank Kokori, Adams Oshiomhole, John Odah, Salisu Mohammed, Lawrence Osagie, Abdulwaheed Omar, Issa Aremu, Brown Ogbeifun, Bayo Ogun, Bayo Olowosile, Phillip Okougbo, Ayuba Wabba, Igwe Achese, Peter Esele, Chris Uyot, Ismail Bello, Joe Ajaero, Aitokhuehi, Macauley, Abiodun Aremu, Denja Yaqub, Ismail Bello, Friday Otono, etc.

Some officials of the Federal Ministry of Labour were quite helpful too; Messrs Chike Okogwu, Bosah, Dr Tunji Oloapa, Dr Koripamo-Agary, Peter Ajuzie, Mrs Braimah, were especially understanding. Some top ex-civil servants were instrumental in preventing some of my less illuminating interpretation of government policies from dominating my writings and thus were refreshing counter-points; Allison A. Ayida (former Head of the Federal Civil Service and Permanent Secretary of Ministries of Finance and of Economic Development at various times), Chief Philip Asiodu, Alhaji Joda, Alhaji Damcida (dubbed 'super permsecs' in 1960s till mid-1970s), and Stephen Agodo (Permanent Secretary in the Cabinet Office, and later co-head of the Nigerian Security Organisation)

I enjoyed conviviality of colleagues at the University of Ibadan where I taught from 1979 till 1983, and especially of Bade Onimode, Bobo Adesomoju, Julius Okojie, Segun Agagu, Segun Ekundayo, Femi Otubanjo, John Ohiorhenuan, Alex Gboyega, Bayo Adekanye, Lai Erinosho, Justin Labinjoh, Sam Olofin, Ibi Ajayi, Godwin Sogolo, Edho Ekoko, Chris Ikporukpo, Olorunfunmi Sonubi, and Morankinyo Omole.

As for Unilag, Professor Olatunde Oloko and Vremudia Diejomaoh were especially accommodating, after the persuasive skills of Professor Ukandi Damachi landed me here from Ibadan, and the Vice Chancellor then, Professor Akin Adesola, most welcoming. Indeed I have been privileged to have had excellent relationship with most vice chancellors since then, especially Professors Omotola, Ibidapo-Obe, Sofoluwe and Ogundipe. Then Professors Uvieghara, Adeyemi, Adeogun, Utuama, Osinbajo, Fogam, Oyebode, Agomo and Omorogbe in the Faculty of Law, and A. Asiwaju and Kenku most gracious. Membership of the Central Research Committee brought me in touch with some stimulating minds; Professors Dele Olowokudejo, Solomon Okunuga, Mustapha Danesi, Rufus Akinyele, Funso Falade, Makanjuola, Ayodele Atsenuwa, Mopelola Olusakin, Ademola Omojola, Solomon Akinboye, Olumide Olusanya, Olukemi Odukoya, Olufunmilayo Adeyemi, Kehinde Olayinka, Abayomi Okanlawon, and Wellington Oyibo. The few senior professors at the time and who all turned out to be Deans of the Faculty of Business Administration (now Management Sciences) have been great builders; Professors Nwankwo, Damachi, Iyanda, Adepoju, Bello and Ojo. Then, of course, all other colleagues in the Departments of Actuarial Science and Insurance, Accounting, Banking and Finance and Business Administration over nearly four decades, too many to mention individually. And it has been with great pride and immense satisfaction to watch the Department of Industrial Relations & Personnel Management (now Employment Relations & HRM) grow from a three-person Department in 1983 to produce nearly thirty academic staff with doctorate degrees and some professors in the bargain as at today.

Over the years, contacts with certain persons have been invaluable: Professor Sam Oyovbaire, Dr Tunji Olagunju, Armen Deukmedjian, Rear Admiral Mike Akhigbe, Joe Idudu, G. G. Darah, Festus Iyayi, and Barnabas Agbonifoh.

Of course, I owe my genes and everything else to the Otobo Family of Uzere, headed successively by Papa Chief William Eboe Otobo, Elder Stanford Otobo, Chief James Ekpre Otobo, and Engr Guy Eboe Otobo.

Finally, I am unable to thank enough Mama, the very beautiful, kind and warm mother, Madam Iledi Bateren-Otobo, and Alero and our children – Kome (Komsy Hurricane Kay), Efena (Efena Babe) and Odafe (SonnyBoy).

Preface

I arrived University of Ibadan's Department of Sociology in 1979 from St Edmund Hall, Oxford, after my doctorate studies to find only a yearly one-week conference for trade unionists and industrial relations practitioners organised by the Department of Adult Education as main popular and formal avenue for imparting what might have been regarded as essentials of trade unionism and labour relations, notwithstanding the very few lecturers specialising in labour economics in two or three universities and the path blazed by Professor T. M. Yesufu. From the 1950s till 1974 when the military regime banned foreign and international labour centres from having affiliate-members in Nigeria, foreign sponsors of Nigerian central labour organisations expended much on such training programmes abroad and locally in respective 'labour schools' or 'training centres' so established by them.

Two foresighted academics, the head of department of sociology, Professor Onigu Otite and Professor Fetuga, Dean of Postgraduate School, embraced my suggestion for a Masters of Industrial and Labour Relations programme, which commenced in 1980 with me as the Co-ordinator, the first of such in Africa. Then Professor Ukandi Damachi nurtured the birth of an Industrial Relations and Personnel Management academic department in 1982 at the University of Lagos that offered both undergraduate and postgraduate degrees which I joined in 1983. Aside from being the first in Africa, it was followed a few years later in the inauguration of a Nigerian Industrial Relations Association (NIRA), a pioneering effort in Africa.

As for the contents of academic courses and intellectual discourses, such were substantially configured by raging debates between and within various 'schools', 'paradigms' and against Marxist and socialist social scientists, largely by-products of the Cold War, socio-economic and technological developments and ideological and political dissensions especially wracking Europe and the Americas over those decades. Such attention that was paid to colonialism, post-colonial states and workers and their organisations therein by the self-defined experts or specialists was largely in relation to their "revolutionary" potentials in a proclaimed world struggle between the East and the West in Cold War parlance, which either party might capitalise on.

In some ways, therefore, the Inaugural Lecture and this book, titled *Of Bushmen and Work: Models, Modelling and Illusions*, might easily pass for a part-journey down memory-lane, reliving some of the debates and their mutations, the attendant images fostered and foisted, and competing presentations of the dynamics of colonial and post-colonial societies till recently. As can be expected, seven decades on from the onset of the Cold War, many "perspectives", "schools", "models", "theories" which had the seeming air of infallibility have become enfeebled, an understatement, by several developments, including the collapse of the Soviet Union and political and economic changes in Europe (read European Union), Asia (especially China, Japan and India) and North America, passions and tendencies unleashed in Europe and the USA over massive migrations in the last twenty years especially have enlarged the scope for the falsification role of facts on the ground and advances in information and communication technology (especially social media these days) playing no small part by contributing to our increasingly more rational evaluation and determination of models or democratic ideals and practices.

This is a small part in the on-going attempt at placing

organisational, managerial and workers practices in Nigeria, if not Africa and elsewhere, into truer perspective.

Abbreviations and Acronyms

ADB	African Development Bank
ADR	Alternative Dispute Resolution
AFL-CIO	American Federation of Labour & Congress of Industrial Organizations.
ALLCCTU	Soviet All-Union Central Council of Trade Unions
ASCON	Administrative Staff College of Nigeria
ASUP	Academic Staff Union of Polytechnics
ASUU	Academic Staff Union of Nigeria Universities
COEASU	Colleges of Education Academic Staff Union
CONMESS	Consolidated Medical Salary Structure
CSR	Corporate social responsibility
CSTWU	Civil Service Technical Workers Union
DGB	Deutscher Gewerkschaftsbund
ECOWAS	Economic Community of West African States
EFCC	Economic and Financial Crimes Commission
EUSS	Elongated University Salary Structure
FME	Federal Ministry of Education
GATT	General Agreement on Trade and Tariffs
HAFSS	Harmonised Armed Forces Salary Structure
HAPPSS	Harmonised Police and Para-Military Salary Structure
HAPSS	Harmonised Public Service Salary Structure
HATISS	Harmonised Tertiary Institutions Salary Structure
ICFTU	International Confederation of Free Trade Unions
ILO	International Labour Organization
IMF	International Monetary Fund
JAMB	Joint Admissions and Matriculation Board
MDAs	Ministries, Departments and Agencies
NARD	National Association of Resident Doctors

NASU	Non-Academic Staff Union of Universities and Allied Institutions
WFTU	World Federation of Trade Unions
NATUV	National Association of Trade Union Veterans
NBTE	National Board for Technical Education
NCCE	National Commission for Colleges of Education
NCE	National Council on Education
NECA	Nigeria Employers Consultative Association
NGOs	Non-Governmental Organizations
NIC	National Industrial Court
NIRA	Nigerian Industrial Relations Association
NLC	Nigerian Labour Congress
NMA	Nigerian Medical Association
NNPC	Nigerian National Petroleum Corporation
NPSNC	National Public Service Negotiating Councils
NSIWC	National Salaries, Incomes & Wages Commission
NUC	National Universities Commission
NUCFRLANMPE	National Union of Chemical Footwear Rubber Leather and Non Metallic Products Employees
NUPENG	National Union of Petroleum & Natural Gas Workers
NUPMTPAM	Nigerian Union of Pharmacists, Medical Technologists & Profession Allied To Medicine
NUT	National Union of Teachers
NUTGTW	National Union of Textile, Garment & Tailoring Workers
OND	Ordinary National Diploma
PENGASSAN	Petroleum & Natural Gas Senior Staff Association
PTI	Petroleum Training Institute
RMAFC	Revenue Mobilisation, Allocation and Fiscal Commission
SAP	Structural Adjustment Programmes
SCIMPEX	Syndicat des Commercents Importateurs-Exportateurs
SEWUN	Steel and Engineering Workers Union of Nigeria
SSANU	Senior Staff Association of Nigerian Universities
SSAUTHRAI	Senior Staff Association of Universities, Teaching Hospitals, Research and Allied Institutions

SSS	State Security Services
TOPSAL	Harmonised Top Public Office Holders Salary
TUC	Trades Union Congress
UGSS	Unified Grading and Salary Structure
UNESCO	United Nations Educational, Scientific and Cultural Organization
UNO	United Nations Organization
WAEC	West African Examinations Council
WCL	World Confederation of Labour
WTO	World Trade Organization

Contents

Introduction

Of Labels and Labelling

Mr Vice Chancellor, Colleagues, Ladies and Gentlemen, the Portuguese, first, and the Dutch later, drifted across the Atlantic Ocean and floated into the area that was later to be christened Cape of Good Hope in present-day South Africa, from the fifteenth century onwards, in their competitive search for an alternative route to India and Asia, their usual route through modern-day Middle East plagued by centuries of all manner of wars, the most devastating being those between mediaeval Christendom and Islamic kingdoms and empires, details of which need not detain us here though are of some relevance to ensuing social distinctions, constituting of self-labelling and labelling of others especially. Dominated and characterised by centuries of repressive, authoritarian theocratic rule, slavery, serfdom, and mass illiteracy, most social labels were predictably more primordial, tribal, with physical existence not only truly nasty, brutish, and short, but also what passed for social consciousness or orientation was dominated by corrosive clash of Christian precepts and more seductive and resilient animism and folklores from the Middle Ages. Class distinctions and accompanying social practices were bald, blunt, degrading and unapologetically dehumanising as only a few were regarded as truly human in our modern conception of it. We are here referring to territories stretching from what was known as Europe to defunct Soviet Union. Some of these illiterate, landless serfs and peasants fleeing political tyranny, poverty and misery in Medieval European cities, kingdoms, principalities and some other political groupings, found their way, initially through the instrument of trading companies but later via direct surplus labour-exportation, to

South Africa and labelled some indigenous African ethnic groups they met "Bushmen".

Now, Mr Vice Chancellor, unlike these lowly European tribesmen, who previously worked their lives out in infested fields, swamps, bushes and forests and under indescribably filthy conditions generally, none of these so-called Bushmen had actually seen a "bush", living freely for centuries in semi-arid, desert conditions, dominant vegetation largely of sand, a few streams and some clusters of grass. That was not really the point under consideration at all in this scenario: the San or Khoi people were declared "Bushmen" metaphorically, held to be and treated as Bushmen-humans-of-a-sort, a perverse but self-serving substitution or reversal of social positioning embedded and rationalised in stereotypes by foreign intruders, of which military subjugation of more and more local populations and attendant politico-administrative arrangements most systematically and ruthlessly elaborated upon, Apartheid its last mutant, right up to the mid-1980s.

The physical, military, social and political subjugation of one group of people by another, near or far subjugators, has been typical of human affairs from as far back as oral and written documentation have been, and such is not exactly the substance of our attention here. But, subsequent economic, social and political outcomes from such subjugation in more recent times bear greatly on our areas of interest, namely development and management of employment opportunities, management of work, working people and their organisations and explanations of order of these arrangements and their likely future directions. But, more narrowly, we shall offer a critique of all these in respect of Nigeria and Africa.

Models, Modelling and Illusions

One outstanding feature of modern life is the takeover from families of formal and mass education by central or State authorities however constituted, its organisation and curricula development notably. Where, like in Nigeria and Africa, such was accompanied by forced use of foreign languages, it should not be too difficult to appreciate more far-reaching impact of formal, mass education as might have resulted, tied, as it has been, to re-ordering of social statuses, types of jobs, compensation regimes and written forms of own histories and cultures. And, as it was a commonplace, colonial powers largely controlled such contents or narratives, into which early generations of local or indigenous elites, teachers, students and academics were fed.

For the Ancient Greeks and Romans, all pre-Mediaeval (and Medieval) European tribes were "Barbarians", but all conquerors have always presented themselves as of superior breed and culture, the colonisation of Africa, Asia, North and South Americas following this predictable tradition. It is this posturing, we urge, that for a variety of self-serving considerations some dominant perspectives on theorising social and political ordering of societies have largely been exercises in *modelling*, that is the mere holding out of certain institutional arrangements and modes of behaviour, prescriptions of a sort, rather than approximations of some prototypes. Indeed, in overwhelming number of cases, we would suggest, if not insist, claimed prototypes are themselves, given the dynamism and unpredictability of human affairs, not transmissible and may not be transplanted, did and do *occur naturally when a combination of certain social, political and economic conditions exists.* Take the example of slavery. Slavery is someone owned by and acting as servant to another, with no personal freedom; a condition of total domination, which historically existed simultaneously everywhere. So did slave riots occur everywhere, existential realities triggering resistance. For slave-owners, brutality would be a virtue, that social contrivance of slavery a mark of enjoying the good life. Fast-forwarding to the late eighteenth and early nineteenth centuries, a circular argument was presented of military conquest or subjugation automatically labelling the subjugated "inferior" and subjugation made possible by the *military superiority* of the subjugator – and *everything* about him or them subsequently. We leave all this for the moment, and shall return to examine the proposition that *outcomes naturally or logically occur when a combination of certain conditions present themselves,* as what has been sketched of slavery, for example, would apply with equal force to practices of patriarchy, matriarchy, wage employment, trade unionism, conflict at work, and so on, enabling us draw out false or otherwise linkages between models, modelling and illusions in the current theorising of work relations in Nigeria, Africa and, sometimes, beyond.

Our use of "model" here is in the sense of "prototype" not *ideal type*, an original on which subsequent copies are based. It is quite usual, in other walks of human and intellectual endeavours, to admit of subsequent copies as possible, if not usually, improvements on the prototype. However in the social sciences, such description of nature of respective societies which claim the prototype-status, especially their economic and political institutions and practices associated with them, have been very slow to admit of this. This slowness, oftentimes refusal to, one here associates with systematic "modelling", which is a rather contrived or skewed description of what constitutes the prototype, also backed by sets of activities and actions, including diplomatic and military pressure, to push other groups and societies into formal proclamation of acceptance of held-out or prescribed specific institutional arrangements. Not only that at this point *prototype* and *modelling* become indistinguishable, copies as *inherently inferior* is decreed but with one revealing exception of copies by *same racial stock* as in North America, Australia, and New Zealand eventually gaining equal status as prototype.

From late-1940s when Soviet Union emerged and the rest of the world was labelled "Western" countries (excepting China from 1948, and Cuba in 1962), the now-famous "ideological" divide and captured by the phrase "Cold War", *modelling*, according to our usage here, by majority of social scientists, diplomats and politicians became something of a duty, but allowing for the possibility of those who could separate differing or dissenting private beliefs from official or formal positions and from those who could not, a distinction which contributes toward the understanding of our use of *illusion* for those entirely mistaken about *models* and *modelling*.

Once *models* and *modelling* merge, and we suggest this has preponderantly been the case in more recent times, the probability of errors in comprehension and analyses increases tremendously, more so in previously colonised areas where formal education and academic analyses have remained substantially externally incubated and influenced. This apparent conflation of model and modelling has arguably spawned various "schools of thought" in many academic disciplines over the last seventy years in particular, a failure to subscribe to some orthodoxy leading to loss of job, stagnation and persecution in several cases in several countries, especially in the USA between 1950s and 1970s.[1] It should albeit be pointed out that seven decades on from the onset of the Cold War, many "perspectives", "schools", "models", "theories" which had the seeming air of infallibility have become enfeebled, an understatement, by several developments, including the collapse of the Soviet Union and political and economic changes in Europe (read European Union), Asia (especially China, Japan and India) and North America that rendered possible an intellectual and academic climate for models and modelling to routinely and increasingly disentangle themselves. These developments, on the whole, seem to have enlarged the scope for the *falsification role of facts on the ground* and advances in information and communication technology (especially social media these days) playing no small part by contributing to our increasingly more rational evaluation and determination of models themselves, their relevance and application to respective societies which claim them, and crucial understanding of how various societies have functioned and mutated in relation to or not to constituents of each so-called model or prototype.

Classical Liberalism and Laissez-Faire Economics

The underlying dictum of the dominant European and North American powers, herein loosely referred as "Western model of economic system", from the late 1880s to late 1930s, is that of leaving the supply of goods and services and the determination of their prices and other terms to the now-famous "market forces", demand and supply. Why? An industrialising Europe was dominated by the doctrine of Classical Liberalism. Classical liberalism holds that individual rights are natural, inherent, or inalienable, and exist independently of government. It is a philosophy that upholds the sovereignty of the individual, with private property rights seen as essential to individual liberty. Applied to

---

[1] Notable cases include Bertrand Russell and Herbert Marcuse who fled Europe for the USA and Angela Davis hounded in California. In American politics, such persecution on ideological grounds or differences was referred to as McCarthyism late 1940s to 1956.

economic matters and general social policy by a group of French, Continental and British economists during and since the times of Adam Smith and David Ricardo, it argues for *minimum* State involvement in the supply or production, pricing and distribution of goods and services. This has since been generally labelled *Laissez Faire Economics*, especially after Adam Smith's books, *The Wealth of Nations* and *The Theory of Moral Sentiments* were published in the eighteenth century and in which, among other things, Adam Smith wrote of an "invisible hand" of the market mechanism, the infallible and most efficient value-allocating role of the forces of demand and supply.

Bringing our attention back to the limits to *modelling*, it did not take long to observe that the capacity of demand and supply to adjust themselves automatically was limited and not as smooth-sailing as propounded, that there were periods of scarcity and that aggregate welfare did not increase as rapidly as claimed. More crucially, like day always following the night or vice versa, period of boom or prosperity for businesses was always followed by period of recession or bust. Karl Marx and his followers, socialists and communists, developed thoroughgoing critique of the "capitalist system", propositions which have all come to be known as the Crisis Theory. The Crisis Theory is concerned with explaining the business cycle, recession and crises in capitalism. Karl Marx noted that it is in the nature of the capitalist economy to suffer from periodic crises because of its *internal contradictions*. Prominent among the contradictions or factors identified by Karl Marx are three, which have remained *classic* and which economists of all ideological hues have come to accept:

a) the tendency of the rate of profit to fall (as more goods and services are supplied because investors increase, prices reduce and profits fall as a result);

b) under-consumption - if the capitalists/employers win the class struggle to push wages down and labour effort up, raising the rate of surplus value (profits), then a capitalist economy faces regular problems of inadequate consumer demand and thus inadequate aggregate demand (fewer employed hands and paid lower salaries than would have been the case and thus less purchasing power and less consumption).

c) full employment profit squeeze - when capital accumulation increases the demand for labour power, thereby raising wages, if wages of the many more employed rise "too high", the wages impact negatively on the rate of profit, which then tends to decline, causing or triggering a recession as investments drop, as labour gets laid off, and declining wages/incomes lead to fall in consumption, which in turn leads to further fall in profits and so on.

Keynesian Economics

At the end of World War II (1944) when all European economies lay in ruins, reconstruction and rehabilitation could not be based on 'market forces' and the activities of private entrepreneurs alone in a situation where capital was very limited and lives extensively disrupted. Helped along by American Marshall Aid Plan, the State in what later became known as Western Europe assumed a commanding role in rebuilding respective economies and which led to the rise and development of the Welfare State. Keynesian Economics are those prescriptions advocated by John Maynard Keynes and economists of his persuasion, measures designed *to assist market forces* rather than give them *complete freedom* as assumed under Laissez Faire Economics.

Keynesian Economics thus attempts a "middle way" between Laissez-Faire, unadulterated capitalism and complete State guidance, to that of partial central control or regulation of economic activity. According to this model, attempts are to address economic crises with the policy of having the State/Government act as:

i) a temporary super-capitalist and pillar of the underlying private enterprise system with its increasing range of welfare policies; and

ii) actively supplying the deficiencies of 'markets' through bailouts, subsidies, incentives, and other palliatives.

Keynesian Economics is thus based on *Economic Planning,* representing an international consensus (that is, essentials agreed under the aegis of the United Nations Organisation which succeeded the League of Nations in late 1940s and Bretton Woods talks that resulted in the creation of the World Bank and the International Monetary Fund and adoption of General Agreement on Trade and Tariffs – GATT- to regulate international trade) on the modification of Laissez Faire Economics, with member-states of the United Nations all adopting "Development Plans" of varying durations (5, 10, 15, etc., years). The model and wisdom now was that *economic development* could be *planned*, and not merely the accidental or unintended, trickled-down effect of unrestrained market forces as under Laissez-Faire regime. So, the "Development Plan" contained a list of projects thought crucial to the development of the economy and increase in aggregate welfare, a few of such presented and slated for completion in a yearly "Budget" and for which funds are voted or sought.

Neo-Liberalism

By early 1970s, the age of economic planning - despite the dramatic increases in mass consumption and rise in living standards in Europe and North America especially - created massive public sectors with huge overheads, stagnating economies with high inflation (stagflation), high taxes and mass unemployment. The theoretical and practical arguments directed at modifying this state of affairs have been labelled *Neo-Liberalism*. Broadly speaking, Neo-Liberalism stands for a set of policies which seeks to transfer part of the control of the economy from the much-enlarged public to the private sector, in the belief that such will produce a more efficient and improved economy (economic growth via more investments, jobs, etc.). The concrete policies advocated under Neo-Liberalism are often taken to be typical in John Williamson's "Washington Consensus". This is a list of policy proposals that appeared to have been adopted by the Washington-based international economic organizations (e.g. IMF and World Bank) and Williamson's list has ten items:

• Fiscal policy discipline; this is designed to help lower expectations for what the government can do to improve the lives of citizens - for example, the policy decision to maintain a reserve of unemployed as part of an inflation-fighting strategy combined with a public relations campaign that this unemployment is natural and cannot be defeated without huge deficits or inflation.

- Redirection of public spending from subsidies ("especially indiscriminate subsidies") toward broad-based provision of key pro-growth, pro-poor services like primary education, primary health care and infrastructure investment;
- Tax reform– broadening the tax base by shifting the tax burden to the middle and lower economic groups and adopting moderate marginal tax rates;
- Interest rates that are market-determined and positive (but moderate) in real terms;
- Competitive exchange rates; rates determined by demand and supply unlike fixed exchange rates imposed under erstwhile Incomes and Policy Guidelines;
- Trade liberalization – liberalization of imports, with particular emphasis on elimination of quantitative restrictions (licensing, quotas, etc.); any trade protection to be provided by law and relatively uniform tariffs;
- Liberalization of inward foreign direct investment including commitment to unlimited transfer of earnings across foreign borders;
- Privatization of State enterprises; the transfer of companies and of the activities of certain parastatals from the public to the private sector, but also in the conversion of social rights into marketable objects. Health and education, traditionally considered to be citizens' rights, become economic interests and, in many countries, are privatised, and purchasing power becoming main determinant of what any citizen may have access. In some cases, remaining public sector agencies and enterprises are encouraged to both adopt commercial and corporate management and organizational structures (e.g. Executive Chairmen in several Nigerian parastatals and agencies) and charge so-called "market rates" for services and products – that is, with privatization of the public sector comes extractive fees for use of such resources as subsidies are eliminated in many areas.
- Deregulation – abolition of regulations that are held to impede market entry or restrict competition, except for those justified on

safety, environmental and consumer protection grounds, and prudent oversight of financial institutions;

- Legal security for property rights; and,
- Financialization of capital – many companies are not able to invest in new physical capital equipment or buildings because they are obliged to use their operating revenue to pay their bankers and bondholders, as well as junk-bond holders. This is what…economy is becoming financialized means. Financialisation is not to provide tangible capital formation or rising living standards, but to generate interest, financial fees for underwriting mergers and acquisitions, and capital gains that accrue mainly to insiders, headed by upper management and large financial institutions. The upshot is that the traditional business cycle has been overshadowed by a secular increase in debt. Instead of labour earning more, hourly earnings have declined in real terms. There has been a drop in net disposable income after paying taxes and withholding "forced saving" for social security and medical insurance, pension-fund contributions and – most serious of all – debt service on credit cards, bank loans, mortgage loans, student loans, car loans, home insurance premiums, life insurance, private medical insurance and other FIRE-sector charges. This diverts spending away from goods and services.[2]

The disciples of free movement of capital, now called 'Neo-Liberals', argued that:

i) development has been blocked by inflated public sectors, distorting economic controls and over-emphasis on capital formation;

ii) governments are part of the problem, not part of the solution; they are inefficient and often corrupt and hence parasitic, not stimulators of growth;

iii) the solution is to privatize most of the public sector;

iv) reduce the scale and scope of government spending; and

---

[2] Hudson, Michael, Financial Capitalism v. Industrial Capitalism (Contribution to The Other Canon Conference on Production Capitalism vs. Financial Capitalism Oslo, September 3-4, 1998)

v) give up all policies, from exchange rate controls to subsidies and redistributive taxation, that alter any prices that would otherwise be set by the impersonal forces of the market.

'Market forces' are now supposed to determine every transaction in the local economy, while the World Trade Organisation (WTO) and similar international rules (which favour the economically more advanced countries) and other tariff and non-tariff obstacles 'regulate' international trade.

Labels in use during various decades since 1940s shall also be deployed here, leaving a critique of some till the end. The prominent ones include "capitalist system", "peripheral capitalism", "under-development", "dependent capitalist state", "neo-colonialism", "prebendalism", "modernisation", "patrimonialism", "neo-patrimonialism", and "patron-clientism".

Finally for this segment, one of the insights from all this, and which has guided our methodology in this Lecture, is the importance of longitudinal studies or surveys, the capturing of the essence of each decade or designated period, its peculiar dynamics rather than a one-fits-all story of a "historically determined" course with its dubious implication of constancy of human behaviour or responses under varying circumstances or conditions.

How far?

That said, we shall now proceed to outline how the Bushmen were organised at work, and how they fared and evaluate some of what has been written about how they fared. Which is to say, Mr Vice Chancellor, our main aim in this Lecture is to bring to the fore the dire need for a re-evaluation of certain species of industrial and labour relations theories in light of Nigerian or African developments. We assume a general familiarity with historical antecedents and of colonialism and its processes and in what became Nigeria. Some knowledge of main concepts and theories in the area of employment and labour relations is also taken for granted. Even at that, the task set before us cannot be accomplished in one swoop, so the more modest attempt is at examining some of the basic assumptions of the *dominant model* of industrial relations as taught in classrooms, trumpeted by government officials, spokespersons for industry, consultants and as reflected in most academic analyses of developments in this field.

More specifically, attention is paid to the behaviour of managerial and non-managerial groups, to incidence of industrial conflict and to other employment relations institutions in colonial and post-colonial periods with the intention of showing important lapses in conventional accounts of the role of the State and of other groups in industrial (employment) relations.

As reflected in State policies, we also contend that many of these policies are on balance defective or wanting as a result of essentially illusory assumption of transfer of relevant institutions (*institutional transfer thesis*) by the colonizer on the part of decision-makers, but more in public sector than in private socio-economic organizations. The *institutional transfer thesis*, it is here argued, is a myth, an *illusion*, which has encouraged a set of policies based on wrong premises and contributing in no small way to the establishment of logically and formally correct (from the adopted perspective) but largely ineffectual institutions on the ground. Most conventional literature seem to perpetuate this myth, an indication of the limited validity and utility of current state of theorising, since such theories fail to relate to, and reflect practice and likely course of development.

We should like to caution again that in this Lecture, one does not attempt a review of different theories of industrial relations, of organizations and of social and industrial conflict nor pretend to cover all aspects of conflict in industry. It is based on the proposition that industrial and work relations as played out in industrialized North America, Japan and European Union especially, stay unlikely to yield significant insights of relevance to our circumstances. *It is not a claim to Nigerian (or African or Asian) "exceptionalism", but a claim to exceptionalism of ALL individual experiences.*

Conceding this latter argument is not to claim that the capacity referred to - derived largely from the activities of multinational companies and other State-organised coercive military, diplomatic and political pressures - could be indefinitely sustained or that current forms of industrial conflict would so interminably persist. The general point here would seem to be that the level of material affluence and aggregate standard of living so far achieved in these economies, the tantalizing physical transformation of cities, and the relatively longer history of "nationhood" and accompanying "patriotism" and "nationalism" (greatly encouraged by world political, cultural and economic domination) have all gone toward influencing the analyses of industrial protests and colouring perceptions of managerial and non-managerial groups alike, and prescriptions offered for "role" of trade unions and other protest groups in society. Here, it will be shown, the model and modelling are starkly moving in different directions.

The Farms in the Bush: How do we go?

The achievement of formal political independence through non-revolutionary means by a great majority of former African colonies and the presence of certain socio-political institutions considered not autochthonous, and attempts by apologists and propagandists for erstwhile colony-owning countries to foist such an impression in the context of the Cold War or rivalry between Western and Communist bloc countries of old would seem to have encouraged the view that the colonized was "groomed" during the colonial situation. And being groomed then implies a 'transfer' of certain ideals, ideas, and institutions as distinct from unintended and largely accidental cultural diffusion resulting from much-expanded contacts, even of the military genre, between different cultures since the thirteenth century or so.

The items commonly asserted as transferred are many, some of which are outside the focus of this Lecture. Nevertheless, they generally centre on socio-political and economic institutional arrangements, along with asserted underlying assumptions. In the political sphere, the obvious would be the relatively modern institution of 'political party' and the liberal ideology of political pluralism. No distinction seems to have been made, in this connection, between 'imitation' or 'emulation' *per se* and *deliberate introduction*, an important distinction one would have thought in light of active discouragement and wholesale suppression of 'politics', of political parties and of democratic political arrangements in the colonies. The economic would include what is described by Macpherson (1962) as 'possessive individualism',[3] and capitalist market relations, especially the institution of private ownership of means of production and distribution (Nkrumah, 1963; Fanon, 1967; Amin, 1973; Arrighi & Saul, 1973; Gutkind & Wallerstein, 1976; Gutkind & Waterman, 1977).

Those who embrace wholesale the institutional transfer thesis are typified by Sir Jefferies (1960) who discussed in amazingly glowing terms the grooming and weaning processes involved in the 'transfer of power' to the colonized.[4] Even in supposedly academic analyses, observed differences between existing practices within the colonies and immediate post-colonial states and the model have been presented as 'deviations' from the British, or French prototype. Professor Hugh Clegg curiously claims, for example, that 'during the last ten years...British possessions have all been subjected to labour legislation drafted as far as possible on British model with the intention of producing a trade union movement with characteristics as close as possible to those of British unions' (1960, 70-1). Peter Kilby (1967) specifically proclaimed, in respect of Nigeria, both the transfer and failure of the 'Anglo-Saxon model of Industrial Relations', characteristically citing the 1938 Trade Union Ordinance, setting up of Whitley Councils, the Factories Act and the Department of Labour's frequent self-reassuring re-affirmation of its preference for voluntary collective bargaining as evidence of such transfer. While in relation to French-speaking African countries, Elliot Berg (1959) is convinced that the French 'passed along their own brand of unionism' with its 'exceptionally rich body of doctrines', 'bequeathing all the ideological heritage of French labour movement' and therefore 'metropolitan imprint remaining strong' (in Galenson, 1959, 215).[5]

---

[3] McPherson, C.B., *The Theory of Possessive Individualism*, OUP, 1962. See also his *Democratic Theory*, OUP, Oxford, 1971.

[4] Jeffries, Sir, *Transfer of Power: Problems of the Passage to Self-Government*, Pall Mall, London, 1960;

[5] The literature here is extensive. The following cover the ground fairly well: Davies, I. *African Trade Unions*. Penguin. 1966: Hodgkin. T. *Nationalism in Colonial Africa*, Frederick Muller, London, 1956 and *African Political Parties*, Penguin, 1961; Morgenthau. R.S., *Political Parties in French–speaking West Africa*. Clarendon Press, Oxford. 1964; Carter. G.C. (ed.), *Political Parties in Africa: Seven cases*. Harcourt, Brace & World. New York, 1966 and *African One-Party States*, Cornell University Press, Ithaca, New York, 1964: and Pfeffermann. G., *Industrial Labor in Senegal*, Praeger, New York, 1968.

In concrete terms, the assumption of institutional transfers seems to underlie the 'technical assistance programmes' and 'projects' of most Western European (now European Union) and North American governments, not to mention the specialized agencies of the United Nations, which involve the use of expatriate 'experts' who are assumed to be indispensable in light of their familiarity with institutions regarded transferred. Windmuller (1963) has noted, in relation to labour organizations, the tendency for external benefactors in 'institutional development programmes' to proceed from a model which almost unfailingly embodies the major characteristics of the institution concerned - structural forms, technologies, hierarchical systems, functions, and so forth - key elements often exported almost in their original form (1963, 569-570).[6] For example, a ministry or department of labour set up in Nigeria by the colonial administration (on the insistence of the Colonial Office in London) is claimed to closely approximate and function like its British equivalent (or parent?), just as similar labour legislation have been interpreted (a la Clegg) to reflect the desire on the part of the Colonial Office in London to establish a British-style trade unionism. Implicit in this approach is that structural forms and functional behaviour are causally related and that structural forms may indeed have a life of their own and thus capable of random transplantation. This may be regarded as the core rationale of the institutional transfer thesis.

Dominant Received Farm-Management Model

The dominant 'received' paradigm or perspective in the social sciences in Africa remains the *systems approach*, neither clearly understood nor elaborated upon in the context of African development and political crises, save for the rather dutiful references to Talcott Parsons as the principal apostle. As vulgarized, the functionalist perspective presents society in terms of 'parts' and 'functions', functional parts that exhibit

---

[6] For a revealing but unbalanced view see Windmuller, J., External influences on Labour Organizations in Underdeveloped Counties, *Industrial and Labour Relations Review* (ILRR), vol. 16. July 1963.

varying degrees of 'functional interdependence' and, conversely, 'functional autonomy'. Although the parts or 'sub-systems' compete for resources, it is expected that they will contribute towards maintaining the system as an on-going entity. It is necessarily assumed that basic consensus prevails about the general configuration of society (whether capitalist or not, prevailing distribution of income and power and so on), that the 'rules of the game', assuming it is actually a game, have been agreed upon and internalized and predictability of actions is assured.[7] Society, instead of being dominated by few antagonistic social classes, is said to boast a multiplicity of interest and pressure groups, and such plurality of associations, it is further argued, ensures diffusion of power and democracy (Roberts, 1959, 1; Dahl, 1967, 24).

Transposed to the industrial relations scene by Allan Flanders (1956) but popularised by John Dunlop (1958), an industrial relations system consists of certain actors, contexts and an ideology which binds the system together. The actors include a hierarchy of managers and their representatives in supervision, a hierarchy of workers (non-managerial) and any spokesman, and specialized governmental agencies (and specialized private agencies created by the first two sets of actors) concerned with workers, enterprises and their relationships. Although Dunlop admits that each actor has its own 'ideology', he insists that these 'ideologies be sufficiently compatible and consistent to permit a common set of ideas which recognize an acceptable role for each actor' (1958, 7 & 17).[8] In Africa where most management are racially and ethnically stratified, aside from other intervening variables, this 'compatibility' of 'ideologies' is severely strained.[9]

Following the pluralist argument, whatever measure of independence trade unions and employers organizations possess would be a function of their ability to protect and pursue their sectional interests within limits of

---

[7] As introductory text see Gouldner, A.W., *The Coming Crisis of Western Sociology*, Heinemann, London, 1968: Merton, R.K., *Social Theory & Social Structure*, Free Press, New York, 1957: and Cohen, S., *Modern Social Theory*, Heinemann, 1968.

[8] Dunlop. J.T., *Industrial Relations System*, S. Illinois Univ. Press, Carbondale & Edwardsville, 1958.

[9] For a critique of the pluralist model in the contest of Britain or economically advanced capitalist states: Miliband, R., *The State in Capitalist Society*. Quartet, 1967: Fox. A., Industrial Relations: A Social Critique of Pluralist Ideology in Child. J. (ed), *Man and Organization*. George Allen & Unwin, London. 1973.

existing conventions and laws. Such laws and regulations themselves are presented as 'fair' or 'neutral', as they are claimed to be outcomes of general consensus or 'bargaining'. The recognition of conflicting interests should logically lead to more systematic settlement of disputes, or in Ralf Dahrendorf's phrase 'routinization of conflict'. Routinization is itself only made possible, according to Dahrendorf (1959), by the creation of certain structural arrangements including 'parliamentary' negotiating bodies in which groups meet, namely institutions of mediation and arbitration, the formal representation of labour within individual enterprise, and the tendency towards an institutionalization of workers' participation in industrial management (1959, 257). This way, the 'institutional isolation of industrial conflict' (from political and other conflicts) would be achieved (ibid.).[10]

Professor Hugh Clegg is to see 'industrial democracy' in terms of three elements, namely: a) that trade unions must be independent both of State and management; b) that only unions can represent industrial interests of workers; and c) that the ownership of industry is irrelevant to good industrial relations (1960, 21). However, as interdependence generates 'cooperation', Clegg further argues, 'collective bargaining is therefore a potent and well-designed mechanism for the protection of interests and rights - the first requirement of any system of democracy' (ibid.).[11]

Collective bargaining, by definition, then rules out *unilateral determination* of terms of employment by any of the parties, nor is it expected to go beyond the thrashing out of details of basic pay rates, overtime, manning and other fringe benefits. This itself presupposes that: a) conflict in industry concerns such issues alone; b) collective bargaining is a 'closed' system, unaffected by external developments since it dwells on internally-generated problems in industry or company; c) there are no external sources of disputes in industry; and d) industrial conflict could be contained within industry, given 'institutional isolation', and other

---

[10] For some details, Dahrendorf. R., *Class and Class Conflict in Industrial Society*, Routledge & Kegan Paul. London, 1959.

[11] Details in Clegg, H.A., *A New Approach to Industrial Democracy*, Blackwell. Oxford, 1960. For a critique, Blumberg, P., *Industrial Democracy: the Sociology of Participation*, Constable, 1960.

constraining factors built into 'parliamentary' character of the institution of collective bargaining.[12]

These various arguments in respect of the dominant industrial relations model may be summarized thus:

a) that the State is but one of many interest groups in society and tends to reconcile conflicting interests (this implies 'neutrality');

b) that trade unions should be pre-occupied with so-called 'bread and butter' issues;

c) that trade unions be apolitical in the sense of no attempts at capturing state power (partisanship might be permitted as Flanders (1979, 39) persuasively argued that 'taking sides is the best strategy because it produces best results');

d) that industrial ownership is irrelevant to good industrial relations;

e) that industrial conflict may arise *over* relatively marginal issues but which paradoxically remain 'central' to interests of workers as such other issues as income redistribution and emergent pattern of economic ownership are either products of consensus or 'necessary' to keep the system going and are, at any rate, beyond the pale of collective bargaining;

f) that collective bargaining as collective approach in industry to sorting out disputes, handling unforeseen and planned developments, and for implementing agreements is not only effective but also largely determines both issues and scope of conflict; and

g) institutional arrangements and relevant legislation approximate a generalized Western model and bodies, such as trade unions, function similarly, enabling wholesale borrowing of solutions and theories.

In what follows, a general critique is developed to indicate the limited applicability and validity of dominant industrial relations model in the context of Nigeria or Africa, revealing the absence of bases for a great many of its assumptions and tenets.

---

[12] For a comprehensive coverage of the concept see Flanders, A. (ed), *Collective Bargaining*, Penguin, 1968.

Harmattan and Farm Management

Colonialism, the Harmattan season, is defined by the *International Encyclopaedia of the Social Sciences* as 'the establishment and maintenance, for an extended time, of rule over an alien people that is separate from and subordinate to the ruling power. Some features of the colonial situation are the domination of an alien minority, asserting racial and cultural superiority over a materially inferior native majority' (vol. 3, 1). This definition might not be the most comprehensive nor most accurate but serves our purpose well enough as the picture that emerges is fairly clear: shared norms and consensus that underpin functionalist explanations of social structure have had little to do with the establishment of the colonial polity or of Nigeria.[13]

We are little here concerned about the details of neither colonial resistance nor the strategies employed to co-opt various elements of the colonized. But we may observe that:

a) whatever the differences in opinion, which are many, over why colonies were acquired in the first place, colonial powers and respective colonial administrations up till 1960s, subscribed to the prevailing capitalist economic ideology of *laissez faire*. As noted earlier, this meant little or no government intervention in economic matters, and the powerful colonial oligopolistic companies not only managed their affairs and the local population as they saw fit, many of them pre-dated colonial administration itself;[14]

b) the establishment of a rudimentary colonial administrative framework and of utilities to provide electricity and water for urban-based Europeans, and construction of rail lines, ports to evacuate mineral and agricultural produce formed the nucleus of the public sector;

c) extensive wage labour force emerged in response to the activities of pre-colonial and colonial companies and administrations. Though relatively small in number because of the limited nature of economic

---

[13] For an incisive treatment see Wallerstein, I. (ed), *Social Change: the Colonial Situation*, Wiley, New York, 1966 and Fanon, F., *The Wretched of Earth*, Penguin, 1973 edn.

[14] The Royal Niger Company, for example, conquered, established and ruled the Southern Protectorate of Nigeria a decade before formal colonial domination in 1900. More details in Dike, O., *Trade and Politics in the Niger Delta*, OUP, 1956 and Ikime, O., *Groundwork of Nigerian History*, Heinemann, Ibadan, 1980.

activities, which centred around mining, trading and export-cropping in selected produce, its impact greatly surpassed its size for colonial society was urban-based and workers in both sectors, with a few exceptions of plantation-dominated colonies, were also concentrated in few towns and cities as existed;

d) that despite different attitudes to colonial possessions,[15] there was striking similarity in colonial labour policies: the use of forced and convict labour in mines and for construction purposes, reluctant payment of low wages much later as labour shortages became quite acute because of mass desertion and wartime military demands, and attempts to subdue local opposition and reduce labour costs by importing labour from other colonies.

A. *Farms and Conflict*

Elegant conceptions of industrial (or any) organization as 'coalition of interests', for example, bear little relation to the 'firms' that operated since the eighteenth century in Nigeria or Africa. Apart from being dubbed 'palm oil ruffians', 'bands of adventurers' and like abusive but revealing labels in the nineteenth century, right up to the 1930s 'firms' or 'companies' were armed groups of men who thoroughly employed and understood the language of violence. Cut-throat competition, exacerbated by national and personal rivalries and indigenous resistance, often rendered 'trading' a more hazardous business than is conventionally understood. It is usual for each company to carve out a zone for itself while organizing military raids against rivals in violation of 'concessions' that passed from hand to hand in metropolitan business circles.

This trade introduced extensive money wages (which co-existed fitfully with the use of cowry shells and manila as medium of exchange right into the twentieth century) and created a pool of ex-slaves and dispossessed persons who clustered around powerful local and foreign traders, and functioned variously as porters, guards, clerks, errand boys

---

[15] Regarded as integral part of France or Portugal or Spain, private possession by Leopold of Belgium and dependent territories by Britain.

and armed thugs as occasion demanded. Remuneration was mostly in kind; food, clothing, spirits, brass and copper bands and other European manufactured metal ware. Private employers and 'workers' were housed in 'company yards' and fully protected by 'company troops'. To speak of workers and industrial conflict at this time would be premature because apart from parts of South America, mining did not actually catch on till the 1870s and well-organized companies did not appear till the 1920s.[16] In relation to Africa, it was a period characterized by massive eviction and annihilation of various indigenous populations and vicious conflicts among settlers, companies and some metropolitan governments over land, mineral rights and territories.

The period between World War I and II ushered in changes in the forms of the 1917-8 Russian Revolution, the formation of League of Nations (and United Nations Organization in 1940s), of the International Labour Office, and nationalist independence movements. These institutions and political movements directed attention to colonial situations, the possibility of political independence, and plight of colonial labour movements and their revolutionary potential as harassed nationalist politicians visibly threw their weight behind indigenous workers' organizations that unwittingly offered legitimate cover when political parties themselves were hardly tolerated.

The 1930s economic depression killed many companies in Nigeria and those that survived became bigger monopolists which, between a handful (in many colonies only one or two) dominated the import-export trade, shipping and finance (Perham, 1948; Hopkins, 1973). Structurally such companies had branches or stores in major cities with their licensed export-crop buying agents strategically located in areas of cultivation. Internal administration and determination of terms of employment for workers in these private concerns, who had begun to emerge in significant numbers, were of little interest to the colonial administrations.

The infrastructural activities of colonial administrations had increased, facilitating the growth of wage labour force in the public sector in spite of widespread use of forced and convict labour. The civil service,

---

[16] In relation to Africa see Lanning, G. & Mueller, M. (ed.), *Africa Undermined*, Penguin. 1979.

police, armed forces, central bank and other institutions which later bore the tag 'parastatals' had use for a permanent labour force with requisite skills and varied levels of competence. It is thus instructive to note that public sector workers were the first to unionize and agitate for better living conditions and other terms of employment. Given their strategic importance in terms of ensuring unceasing flow of essential raw materials to metropolitan industries, the obvious need to maintain an administrative apparatus and corollary interest in 'law and order', public servants could not be prevented for too long from forming trade unions or associations.

Industrial conflict, especially strikes and though poorly organized at the beginning and restricted to lower-statused workers and labourers, occurred mostly during war periods when inflation was accompanied by shortages of essential food items, many of which, like salt, were imported. Indeed, there were general labour rebellions in most British colonies in late 1920s and 1930s, Nigerians and other Africans had since 1902 been protesting against discrimination in pay and other conditions of employment in favour of Europeans who, largely steeped in racism and superiority complex, held better paid and more prestigious positions irrespective of qualifications, skills, age and experience (Yesufu, 1962; Ananaba, 1969).

Industrial dissent on part of indigenous clerical workers (mainly clerks in civil service, companies and teachers) was more muted and restricted to petitions bearing heavy moral overtones. Labourers and other artisans had more frequent recourse to strikes and other more effective forms of industrial conflict, being worse off in status and security of employment. Colonial administrations tended to tolerate petitions from white-collar workers being less threatening, while troops and police were freely used on labourers and other categories of workers in both private and public sectors. Striking workers were held to disturb 'public peace', and certainly 'politically-motivated' and 'communist-inspired', from colonial officialdom's jaundiced point of view, with the upsurge of nationalist movements for political independence especially from the mid-1940s in Nigeria.[17]

Such arbitrary use of force to suppress workers and industrial dissent was sometimes denounced in motley social circles in metropolitan base, especially when lives were lost and given publicity. Labour rebellions and effects of the 1930s economic depressions encouraged greater metropolitan involvement in colonial economies. As reflected in policies, colonial administrations were pressurized into establishing negotiating machinery, enacting labour codes and other protective legislative pieces to direct trade unions into politically safer channels. Such pressure was contained in British Lord Passfield's (Colonial Secretary) 1930 Dispatch to all colonial governors which lamented the 'lack of safety valves' in labour policies and, as interpreted by Professor B. C. Roberts, 'such might give rise to extremist organizations that might become politically active' (1964, 183). Colonial 'labour policy' therefore involved the task of monitoring political dissent and revolutionary potentials, part reaction to the fright still being generated in Europe by the 1917-8 Bolshevik Revolution and emergence of Soviet Union and Eastern European countries.

These attempts at influencing and re-channelling colonial workers responses and directing their organizations by metropolitan officials, colonial administrations and employers, who drew upon certain administrative and legal devices, applied with limited success to metropolitan situations themselves, are what have been said or claimed to represent or constitute 'institutional transfers'! For example, the British government got colonial administrations to introduce but unsuccessfully 'Whitley Councils' in the 1940s as negotiation platforms in the public sector of several colonies. Originally introduced in Britain itself only in 1911, failed to make any impact, as in the colonies, and were discontinued soon afterwards (Flanders, 1972, 129-130).

The introduction of 'labour officers', 'trade union officers' and 'trade union cadres' to directly influence labour leaders has generally been

---

[17] Such arbitrariness in the case of Africa has been documented by Davies, I., *African Trade Unions*, Penguin, 1966: Berg., E. & Butler. J., Trade Unions in Coleman. J. & Rosberg. C.G. (eds.). *Political Parties and National Integration in Tropical Africa*, Univ. of California Press, Berkeley and Los Angeles, 1964.

misleadingly interpreted to mean introduction of *purveyors* of metropolitan brand of unionism, when evidence points to refusal by colonial employers to adopt 'collective bargaining' as a method of sorting out some differences and trade union and labour officers remained part and parcel of colonial administration's repressive and surveillance apparatus (Davies 1958 & 1966). As late as the 1950s in Nigeria, the colonial administration was forced to openly admit in respect of the private sector that 'some stoppages of work which occurred might have been prevented if adequate means of consultation between the management and the workers had existed' (Annual Report, 1953, 24). Such intense employer hostility was also partially reflected in the suppression of unionism in the private sector which in Nigeria did not establish strong roots till the 1960s after Independence.

It might be useful to note in addition that some of the companies were more powerful than individual colonial governors or administrators themselves. The Laissez-faire doctrine aside, the companies' links with powerful political and industrial circles in Europe were often used to influence the *choice* of governors and of personnel to other important positions. For instance, Captain (later Major, Colonel and Lord) Lugard was an employee of the Royal Niger Company, commanded the company's troops, moved up to be the commander of the West African Frontier Force, and then Governor of Nigeria. The companies as such were a 'state within a state', and in jointly-owned mines (e.g. tin mines in Jos) and plantations with the State, the colonial administration habitually furnished forced and convict labour.[18] Draconian labour laws and war-time emergency regulations ensured free use of law-enforcement agents to break strikes, just as industrial and other domestic policies kept out other rival European firms. To this extent, the interest of British companies and administration often coincided, rendering meaningless the claim of 'neutrality' and conflicting-interest regulating role of the State as contained in the pluralist doctrine earlier discussed. Perhaps, more importantly from the professed attributes of 'collective bargaining' and mutual recognition of interests enabling 'routinisation of conflict' to

---

[18] Freund, B. *Capital and Labour in Nigerian Tin Mines,* Univ. of Ibadan Press, Ibadan, 1981

come to pass, neither colonial administration nor employers saw trade unions or any other segment (with the exception of 'chiefs', '*emirs*' and '*obas*' appointed by colonial officialdom) of the populations as representing legitimate interests. If union leadership did not represent workers interests, workers themselves denied of rights, and operations of their organizations severely curtailed and monitored, no negotiating machinery, strikes broken by troops and police, all this would seem a far cry from Dunlop's famous three sets of actors in his system of industrial relations with mutual balancing of interests and shared norms and values.

The intensification of ideological rivalry between and among groups of European states and attendant 'Cold War' riveted attention of both metropolitan and colonial administrations on trade union leadership and nationalist politicians. The politics of decolonization proceeded with 'Africanization' of various positions in civil services and other arms of the State, with the notable exceptions of Spanish and Portuguese authorities who still persisted in the myth of colonies as 'overseas provinces'. And even where political and social developments did not explode into widespread and organized violence as did in Kenya (Congo, Guinea Bissau, Angola and Mozambique much later), trade unionists were especially hounded by security forces and employers did as they pleased; after all, in the context of their anxieties for profits and existing economic arrangements, striking workers could only be 'potential communists', instigated by nationalist politicians from their jaundiced reckoning.

Be that as it may, in late 1950s a few of the bigger companies conceded a measure of recognition to workers and their organizations but which suffered one grave weakness, namely their reliance on 'advice' from metropolitan centres or headquarters during crucial negotiations. Roberts & de Bellecombe (1967, 43) have noted that:

> In the former Federation of French West Africa most trading and commercial enterprises were members of the Syndicat des Commercents Importateurs-Exportateurs (SCIMPEX). The control exercised over the policy and actions of SCIMPEX was quite rigorous. Any agreement that it might propose to make on wages or any other matter was subject to approval from Marseilles or Paris. It was, in fact, impossible for even a detail

to be modified without the securing of telegraphic authorisation from France.

This 'teleguidage' or 'remote control' was hardly peculiar to French companies for Lord Lugard had deplored in 1914, in respect of British companies in Lagos, their habit of giving 'colourless reply' to official query while 'consulting their principals in England' (Report on Amalgamation, 1920, 34-5). That teleguidage of companies hampered negotiations and readiness to reach a compromise can hardly be doubted. The more important point here is that, on top of all the overwhelming odds against workers and their organizations within the colonies, 'collective bargaining' really involved managements in Europe too! Not much 'bargaining' or 'negotiations' could have been taking place and which would seem to partly explain why workers readily used the strike weapon, compelling managements within and without to yield on some grounds by exploiting adverse publicity that would accompany industrial action, following predictable over-reaction on the part of law enforcement agencies and loss of profits due to disruptions in production or trading and boycott by local population of retailed European consumer goods as was widely the case.

B. Farming Disagreement Processes

The wage earning labour force was small, largely urbanized and organized around individual companies or branches thereof. The associated problem of small size of unions condemned most to financial stringency, more so as not all members paid their dues. This also meant from limited to no 'strike' funds, and a consequence was that trade unions could not sustain a prolonged strike if financial resources were the only criterion. Eliot Berg (1959, 226) has a graphic description of a typical strike situation in the colonies:

> ...considerable discipline is exhibited during these stoppages. It is ordinarily not prudent for an African to present himself for work during these protest demonstrations. Racial alignments

become crystal clear; Europeans are almost at work and Africans are not. On both sides it is something of an act of treachery to desert one's racial camp. Often the protest tends to become generalized, starting as a demonstration against a decision of the employers or administration...Thus during these protest demonstrations the African urban community tends to close its rank. Ethnic particularism and union ideological differences tend to be submerged in the common African struggle against the European employers and administration.

Despite the scenario outlined above, the impact of strikes and protest was undoubtedly limited, except during war periods. For one thing, unions were not capable of forcing employers to shut down however widespread the work stoppage because of presence of Europeans in key positions. This was reinforced by the ease with which employers could break strikes in a labour market characterized by oversupply and a relatively undifferentiated and non-industrial economy. In addition, the breaking of strikes under emergency powers of the administration, which preceded 'negotiations', frequently resulted in the death or banishment of trade union leaders and demise of unions. The destruction of unions could also be seen in official figures as fewer stay on the list from year to year having been de-registered, *a labour-control weapon that has no parallel in Britain and therefore could not have been 'transferred'*.

Furthermore, the situation as described by Berg (1959) clearly shows the remarkable little success achieved in the 'institutional isolation of industrial conflict' from political or other forms of conflict as propounded by Ralf Dahrendorf (1959). Routinization of conflict in this case had more to do with pervasiveness, not cognition paid opposing claims so as to reduce conflict to mere symbolism or ritual. Finally, the ownership of industry has turned out after all, much against Professor Clegg's postulate, not irrelevant to good industrial relations.

C. Town Hall Meetings in the Public Farms

War conditions, as in Europe, dispelled more than a few myths about nature of management and its functions. The necessity to ensure cooperation of workers compelled employers in both sectors to meet many of workers demands, which included collective determination of size of profits. 'War bonuses' were granted and thereafter in British and French colonies, commissions were established after particular nasty conflicts. Experts were also sent to the colonies who recorded their impressions and made recommendations, some of which were implemented. Generally colonial administrations attempted to influence events in the following ways:

a) provided close control over the internal activities of trade unions through the Registrar of Trade Unions who had powers to compulsorily register and de-register unions; the norm was the de-registration of unions involved in strike action);

b) established statutory wage determination machinery by forming 'wages councils' or committees for various departments and industries (which were largely ineffective):

c) imposed compulsory arbitration in some instances while legally forbidding workers in 'essential services' from going on strike, a category that was extended to cover many more sectors of the economy as protests became more widespread and effective: and

d) detached white collar workers from the rest of the proletariat by encouraging them to form 'staff associations' and 'works committees'.

The Civil Service Union always tended to present a long list of demands or grievances to colonial governors, petitioning metropolitan governments proper upon dissatisfaction with local official response. Some commissions found colonial administrations on the wrong, which triggered more protests as such administrations either disputed the findings or delayed implementation of awards. In the very formal sense, 'negotiations' did not actually take place as conditions of employment were contained in civil service orders or documents and stream of guidelines from the Colonial Office in London. Given the 'civilizing mission syndrome' and endemic paternalism of expatriates, indigenous public servants had no points of reference except existing racially-based inequality in pay and fringe benefits which understandably fuelled initial protests. And as settlers and expatriates civil servants sought even better standards of living and colonial administrations compiled their own cost of living indices to justify wage policies, these were themselves to form part of grievances as inflation undermined real earnings; in which case petitions were usually presented to the governors above the head of top civil servants or secretary to the government.

D. Farming Meetings in the Private Farms

Employers in the private sector dispensed with either dispute procedures or collective bargaining (or agreements) for as long as they could in spite of Trade Union Ordinances or Labour Codes and increasingly effective strikes. Where unions existed there still remained the problem of *recognition* by employers. In the British tradition as Professor Roberts has pointed out, 'union recognition has always been a voluntary matter. Employers have been legally free to recognize or not to recognize a union for bargaining purposes: they are also free to make union membership a condition of employment or refuse to employ any person who belongs to a union' (1964. 49-50). Accepting the legal existence of unions without accrediting bargaining status would seem a roundabout way of denying the fact of their representing an interest group, a glaring negation of the main tenet of the pluralist doctrine and of claims of Western democratic principles.

Granted the dehumanizing effects of slavery and slave trade, viciousness of colonial conquest and paternalism and hardly disguised racism of settlers and colonial officials, employers were in no great hurry to extend recognition to a 'band of natives' conveniently held to be aping one of supposedly European institutions. In French colonies, indigenous workers were required to join branches of metropolitan unions, and negotiations were carried on above their heads. Much later and after a series of strikes and mass protests, the French Overseas Minister imposed minimum wages by administrative fiat (Davies; 1966, 90). The closest British equivalent policy would be Wages Boards that sought to establish 'reasonable wages' in several industries, especially in *unorganized* establishments.

As employers moved closer to nationalist politicians as prospects for political independence brightened appreciably, remote control of companies intensified as anxieties over future of investments commensurately increased. Employers commonly encouraged workers to form 'associations' and 'house unions' around branches of their companies as earlier mentioned, and which not only made it manifestly easier for them to influence workers' demands but also rendered such organizations mere conduits for managerial decisions. Most became bodies in which pro-management or cowed officials explained management policies to and informed workers about kinds of expectations they could legitimately hold and aspire to. The combined amalgam of paternalism and assimilation ruled out collective bargaining, producing a crop of workers who genuinely regarded with awe and intense admiration white collar positions, as success symbol. This would seem to be why active unionism in private sector in Nigeria only gained ascendancy (excepting banking and petroleum industries) as from late 1960s. That manual workers and other artisans broke away to form their own organizations in 1930s could be put down to the timidity and conservative bent of leadership of Civil Service Union and of other white collar unions at the time, and higher status enjoyed by clerks and other white collar groups in a colonial perking order.

The Bush, Farmers, Farm Managers and Disagreements in Post-Harmattan Period

A. The General Overseer

The pattern of economic ownership did not change appreciably in the post-colonial period in Nigeria, as in other countries, till only recently. Aside from few socialist-oriented African countries, foreign ownership increased even in the poorest of them. Economic ownership has assumed greater significance in view of the general poverty and the so-called revolution of heightened expectations among the teeming millions. Decades of 'economic planning', of 'development plans', of 'foreign aid' and 'foreign investments' and 'technical assistance' have not achieved any major breakthrough in the development effort. Foreign economic ownership and repatriation of, otherwise domestically investible, profits abroad and level of foreign reserves have all become critical issues in the political economy of these areas in view of mounting foreign debts and adverse terms of trade.

In the first place, most of the elites that came to positions of power through politics of decolonization were not predisposed, conceding ideological orientation and self-interest, to substantially alter pattern of economic ownership save in the sense of increased share of profits accruable to sections of selfsame: the various 'Africanization' and 'indigenization' policies were designed to achieve this limited objective. The importance of this lies in the patently anti-labour policies and legislation, being a reflection of the composition of the State itself, though not a static situation.

It is increasingly held and persuasively argued by some that the configuration of the post-colonial State and its internal politics would seem largely dependent on activities of multinational companies, struggles between fractions of the elites for privileges and 'left overs', workers' and peasants' reactions, and interventionist policies of Western governments (Alavi, 1974; Amin; Arrighi & Saul, 1973; Gunder Frank, 1969).[19]

In many of these countries, and all over Africa specially, business and politics are inseparable, the latter being the quickest means to amassing personal wealth and fortune (Sandbrook, 1974: Dudley, 1973: Fanon, 1973).[20] The political parties are invariably made up of businessmen, professionals and some traditional rulers, and the non-abuse of office is a

---

[19] This is the main theme of the 'dependency school' in development studies. The cited works are Alavi, H., 'The State in Post-Colonial Societies', New Left Review. vol. 24. 1974; Amin, S., Unequal Development, Harvester, Hassocks. 1976 but French edition published in 1973 Arrighi,G. & Saul. J.S., Essays on the Political Economy of Africa, Monthly Review Press. New York & London, 1973: SAUL, J.S., The State and Revolution in Eastern Africa. Heinemann, London, 1979: and Frank. A.G., Capitalism and Underdevelopment in Latin America, Monthly Review Press, New York & London. 1969.

[20] Practically each and every serious study of these areas has documented this self-enrichment process by the political class. Cited works are Sandbrook, R.. Proletarians and African Capitalism, Cambridge University Press. 1971; Dudley.B.J., Instability and Political Order: Politics and Crisis in Nigeria, University of Ibadan Press, 1973: and Fanon, F.. The Wretched of the Earth, op. cit. Practically each and every serious study of these areas has documented this self-enrichment process by the Political class. Cited works are Sandbrook.R., Proletarians and African Capitalism, Cambridge University Press. 1971; Dudley, B.J., Instability and Political Order: Politics and Crisis in Nigeria. University of Ibadan Press, 1973: and Fanon.F., The Wretched of the Earth, op. cit.

rarity and normally would involve award of contracts to own companies or 'front men', inflated contract prices incorporating 'side-kicks' or 'commission', distribution of import licences to friends when such was the policy and outright embezzlement of public funds. Paying due recognition to the fusion of politics and business, the degree of legal regulation that government can establish can only but be minimal. The traditional weapons, such as budgetary policy, progressive taxation, meaningful direction of public investments, location of industry, corporate tax and import restrictions, are all severely undermined by shoddy implementation or non-implementation, corrupt practices of relevant bureaucrats and authorities, and pressure exerted by employers and their organizations and those emanating from Western governments with interests in these economies. It has also been the case, with the counter-productive and misguided intention of 'creating favourable climate for investments', that governments of these poverty-ridden countries in addition do exempt many companies from all manner of taxes and duties, in some cases underwriting losses for the first five or ten years.

Most government's revenues are derived from activities of foreign companies, whether in the form of royalty, taxes or custom and excise duties. This pecuniary link is reinforced by job opportunities provided for a few hundreds (thousands in the case of larger economies). As Miliband (1969) noted in respect of Western capitalist countries, even more applicable to these poorer countries, bureaucrats and other state functionaries do honestly see the survival of these companies, within the logic imposed by dependent structures of their economies, as a large component of the 'national interest'. It could be argued, with considerable justification that this disposition seems less defensible in much of Africa where such companies are largely foreign-owned or controlled, and through such strategies as transfer pricing, high depreciation rates, exorbitant consultancy and technical assistance fees, and profit repatriation, colossal sums of money are continuously siphoned out.

The relevance of all this to industrial relations theory should not be missed: the context within which the State operates remains crucial in understanding its ultimate 'role'. A critical issue here would be the implications of external economic control for domestic socio-economic policies. The logic of their position has pushed most of these governments into greater admiration for repressive colonial labour policies which are now adopted with gusto. As an example, the 'essential services' category has been extended in Nigeria to embrace most workers in the public sector, and much of the private sector too. In the more oppressive African countries over time (Gambia, Burundi, Rwanda, Uganda, South Sudan, Ivory Coast, Democratic Republic of Congo, Liberia, to mention just a few) such legal niceties are discarded for indiscriminate suppression of protests of any kind. Strikes, if not banned, the right to undertake them is so hedged as to make undertaking them hazardous.

Trade unions are still registered and de-registered where not forbidden and arbitrary detention of union officials, especially during strikes remains unparalleled even by colonial standards. And as earlier indicated, in the French-speaking countries (in one or two English-speaking also) one-party governments have, with varying success, interpolated trade unions into the state system, a far cry from the 'rich French tradition' Berg (1964) had thought transferred. From mid-1960s, state structure has been compounded by the rash of military coups, dramatically intensifying privations of labour and eliminating any distinction between political and industrial conflict.

B. Farms, Thorns and Hazards

Some of the industrial organizations, in terms of complexity, rival any in Europe or North America. These organizations have by practice and in protection of certain operations and secrets, attempted to perpetuate right of European members of management to exclusively determine and allocate tasks. Implicit in this is the hardly expressed assumption that such companies being historically European in origin are best run by Europeans. Whatever the merits of such a position, it has been fairly easy to discern that European members of management have varied social backgrounds, skills and formal qualifications, measuring unfavourably against indigenous counterparts in many instances, and yet make up top echelons of organizations. The gross disparities in remuneration and other fringe benefits, as in colonial situation, have caused a great deal of dissatisfaction among Nigerian or African members of management, making predictable their demands for indigenization of top positions.

Indigenization policies or programmes, where adopted as in Nigeria since mid-1970s, have tended to create problems of sorts as companies are now required to strike a delicate balance between quality of personnel and ethnic/racial composition of staff, ethnic chauvinism being both residual product and instrument of inter-elites rivalries. Such ethnic balancing has paradoxically become more acute in totally indigenized establishments as discussed below, exacerbated by partisan attitudes and actions of departing expatriates on whose preferences and intrigues Nigerian or African counterparts partly depend to move up into key positions.

There are three dimensions to resultant tension and state of conflict from the situation outlined above:

a) where management is racially mixed, differentials in along racial lines tend to elicit hostile reaction at this level, often transmitted down to lower employees. The situation is made worse by the tendency on the part of expatriates to monopolise access to essential information about operations of the organization;

b) in totally indigenized establishments ethnic sympathies seem always invoked over issues as recruitment into middle and higher rungs of management, selection of personnel for training and promotion, all breeding acrimony, cliques and factionalization;

c) such differences may be transmitted onto the generality of the labour force and, more importantly, in the classic case of labour-management conflict it is a familiar tactic by personnel managers and general management to exploit racial and ethnic affiliations. Such strategy may be adopted to turn workers against a section of management (say, European or Indian members) or simply to weaken workers resolve to back up their demands by work stoppages, and/or to dilute demands. Where European members of management are indisputably discriminatory, it is not uncommon to find their African colleagues covertly, and sometimes openly, pitching their tents with rest of the workers, successfully 'politicising' the situation by involving bureaucrats or politicians on some occasions.[21]

Many of the indigenously-owned and operated commercial concerns tend either to be ephemeral or spasmodically active. This may be attributed to the fact of being mostly dependent on patronage of larger concerns (subsidiaries of multinational companies especially) and the State (parastatals, development projects, armed forces requirements, police, etc.). Basically these enterprises sprang up as distribution outlets for all sorts of imported secondary and consumer items, servicing and maintenance functions, and in response to indigenization policies and government's contracts. The contraction of the labour force through lay-offs and redundancies because of 'poor climate of investment' and recessions or 'economic downturns', has been rampant in recent times, often accompanied by substantially futile workers protests that easily ran out of steam through lack of sustained support. Trade unionism is suppressed in many of them, while pay irregular. In the construction industry, for example, workers have been known to do without pay for months, the relatively uncomplicated nature of their tasks and migratory nature of such labour, ready availability of substitutes, and indifference of relevant State authorities to their plight with the government itself likely falling back on its payments for already completed contracts all ensure very little resistance by workers in this sector.

The various arms of the Nigerian State themselves have become dumping grounds for varied labour, reflecting employment policy as moulded by regional and private political interests. The unintended consequence of rivalry among regional and ethnic interests has been a proliferation of positions at all levels and consequent over-manning, gross under-utilization of capacity and inefficiency. The bureaucracy and local government have metamorphosed into sprawling structures, an infectious condition also spreading to parastatals created by successive governments (both federal and state) to undertake provision of such services as potable water, electricity, postal and telecommunications and rail, road and air transport before structural adjustment programmes

---

[21] In fact, where expatriates have been accused of 'sabotage' or 'spying' some have undergone interrogation by security agents, a few held incommunicado for days.

(SAP) from mid-1980s, services that are now mostly outsourced and/or privatised. Countries such as Nigeria with a bit more revenue from crude oil sales have undertaken massive investments in many sectors, just as corresponding indigenisation drives have increased scope of State's economic activities and blurring the distinction between public and private sector to a certain extent.

In all, the State has become the biggest single employer and this has had several consequences, the most obvious being concern over size of wage bill and fringe benefits. This concern is manifested in several ways, all equally capable of inducing industrial conflict in the public sector, sometimes spilling over to the private sector. There was the attempt at statutory regulation of wages via perennial and poorly implemented incomes policy from the mid-1980s till late 1990s that unfailingly tended to keep wages down (a wage freeze or wage increases pegged at a norm of anything between five and ten per cent) while urban rent and prices of other items increasing at a quarterly rate of more than 25 per cent. The peculiar logic of incomes policy further pushing the government into intervening in union affairs by passing restrictive laws governing their conduct and further reducing level of legal protection afforded workers. Succeeding deregulation and privatisation policies do not appear to produce less State involvement nor change direction of policies to any appreciable degree; inflation rising as real wages decline and unfavourable exchange rates persistently devalue externally earned revenue.

Great apprehension is also shown over prevailing rates in the private sector, not only for their 'demonstration effect' on public sector employees but also because some of these companies are permitted to pass on 'operating costs' to the State where it owns controlling shares or as 'incentive' to investors; the percentage that goes to 'wages' therefore remains an important consideration. And flowing from the following is the desire on the part of relevant State institutions to minimize occurrence of industrial conflict. A most favoured measure is outright banning of strikes and related activities, complemented by compulsory arbitration under a governmental body (arbitration panel, industrial or military court). The continuous harassment and detention of union officials would seem to be part of 'collective bargaining'.

C. Tending of all Thorns

It would appear that the structure of public administration hardly anticipates conflict at work. The use of confidential reports by superiors for promotion purposes is regarded as sacrosanct, and hierarchies remain quite rigid with privileges ('entitlements') jealously guarded. The possibility of dissatisfaction on the part of bureaucrats or personnel does not appear to have been envisaged hence no standing procedures, in many instances, for periodic review of salaries and other terms of employment. It is perhaps hoped that annual increments and expectations of promotion would suffice. Except civil servants formed trade unions and compelled government to undertake a general review of wages and salaries, the constant erosion of real wages is perhaps expected to be stoically borne. Unionization in the public sector and workers protests would rightly be regarded as having given birth to wages commissions or general wage increases by administrative fiat (Otobo, 1985). The niggardly implementation of such awards would then lead to further strikes, the other reason being the fact that such general wage review also involved re-grading and thus compression or enlargement of existing differentials to which affected workers react. In many of the poorer countries where the bureaucracy dominates the body politic, governments have fallen on this score. The military regimes, while receptive to demands of bureaucrats and in fact, make them comfortable before such demands are presented, tend to viciously suppress strikes and other workers.

The State's arbitration and conciliation services, where they exist, are utilized by both a few private and public employers. Through the relevant ministry, 'guidelines' are laid down against regulating overt forms of conflict in industry. The declaration of a 'trade dispute' is required by law in Nigeria, a 21-day period during which attempts are supposed to be made by all involved to peaceably resolve particular dispute. Upon failing workers and employer could both go on strike and lock out employees respectively, or refer the case to arbitration panel. Quite often the government declares such a strike either 'illegal' or against 'national interest', the police arresting union officials: on some occasions the minister for employment, labour and productivity could pre-empt all by unilaterally referring the case for arbitration. Other 'parliamentary' and tripartite bodies (e.g. Wages and Labour Advisory Boards, Labour or Industrial Courts, Productivity, Prices and Incomes Board) exist where representatives of State organs, of workers and employers periodically meet to ostensibly exchange views and advise policy-makers on current problems and projected legislation. Aside from labour or industrial courts, these bodies have exercised minimal restraining influence over conflict in industry: indeed, it could be argued that the Prices, Productivity and Incomes Board (PPIB) of the 1970s and 1980s might have generated more problems for industry and workers than expected because of its long history of badly implemented incomes policies, more noted for pushing prices upwards. In 2005, the Nigerian government unilaterally 'reformed' a previously voluntary and tripartite National Industrial Court into a unitary one, usurping the right to appoint judges to it and meeting demands of such judges to be placed at par with counterparts in the main judiciary.

In the private sector, employees, especially lower-placed employees, are legally not part of the firm and their mode of participation is generally established by contract of employment. As a majority of workers in industrial establishments are unorganised, disputes procedures, if any, are dictated by management as instanced by Paul Lubeck (1975) in his study of some such establishments in Kano.[22] For organized establishments disputes and grievance procedures may well have been laid down before unions emerged, and more than a few disputes have arisen over cumbersome and long-drawn out nature of such procedures. Few managements in manufacturing make allowance for shop stewards (electronics sector dominated by largely Asian and Levantine managements as greatest culprits), foremen assuming such functions in addition. It would be close to the truth to assert that most employers have tended to look up to State officials and their agencies to take care of major workers protests and demands, such as institution of legal minimum wage, pension schemes, and extension of medical facilities, on company's expense, to families.

---

[22] Paul Lubeck has a good piece on unorganized establishments in Kano. See his chapter in Sandbrook, R. & Cohen, R.(eds.).*The Development of An African Working Class*, Longman. London, 1975.

D. The Farmers-Hunting Strangers

Developments within respective labour movements, typically from 1945 to mid-1970s, have sometimes generated internal squabbles leading to factionalization. The various attempts by "Western" and "communist-controlled" international labour organizations, such as the World Federation of Trade Unions (WFTU), International Confederation of Free Trade Unions (ICFTU), and World Confederation of Labour (WCL), at controlling trade union leaders and labour organizations have created problems of sorts.[23] These efforts have been supplemented by activities of foreign national labour centres (e.g. American AFL-CIO, British TUC, All Soviet C.C.T.U., Israeli Histadrut, and West German DGB) and labour attaches in respective diplomatic missions. The use of scholarships, financial grants and other material incentives has served to create schisms in sundry labour movements. Numerous (usually two or three) local central labour organizations compete for affiliate status of individual trade unions, and it is not uncommon to find a split in union executives over which centre the organization should affiliate to. A resultant factionalization, among other effects, would present problem of recognition for managements, some of which have exploited such situations by withholding some entitlements including membership dues) and even refuse to negotiate a new agreement arguing the unrepresentativeness of both factions of the union. The number of strikes caused by factionalization at central and union level have considerably tapered off in recent times, partly due to governments policy on international labour organizations, as the case in Nigeria when they were banned in 1975, and union leaders own determination to prevent international affiliation issue from further weakening the labour

---

[23] For these organizations and their activities: Kassalow, E. M., *National Labour Movements in the Post World War*, Northwestern University Press, Evanston, 1963: Jacobson, H. K.. 'Ventures in Polity Shaping: External Assistance to Labour Movements in Developing Countries' in Cox, R. (ed.). *International Organization: World Politics*. Macmillan. 1969: Levinson, C., International Trade Unionism, Allen & Unwin, London. 1972: Lorwin,L.L.. The International Labor Movement. Harper. New York. 1953: Lynd, G. E.. *The Politics of African Unionism*. Praeger. Nov. York. 1968: Meynaud, J. & Salah-Bey. A., *Trade Unionism in Africa*. Methuen. London. 1974: and a heavily biased coverage. Lichtblau, G.E. Communist Labor Offensive in Former Colonial Territories," *Industrial and Labour Relations*, vol. 15, April 1962.

movement.[24] Both central unionism and international unionism appear to have moved beyond this acrimonious stage, the latter taking the shape of sectoral organising, for example, the IndustriALL formed in 2012, brought together affiliates of the former global union federations of International Metal Workers Federation, International Federation of Chemical, Energy, Mine and General Workers Union and International Textiles Garment and Leather Workers Federation.[25]

And in cases of widespread work stoppages a divided central leadership has consistently failed to correctly articulate interests of workers. Not surprising, governments and private employers have found it convenient to reach agreements with the more pliant of such leadership faction, while castigating others as 'radical' or 'threat to national security', descriptive labels that presage surveillance and harassment of such by security agents. The detention of such labour or union leaders triggers more strikes until government is forced to release them or totally suppress workers as in one-party states. The important point to note here is that in such conflict situations negotiations take place at national level in countries such as Nigeria, above the heads of individual companies, and between representatives of government and labour unions before employers are formally brought into the picture. Oftentimes the government is compelled to 'sell' to the employers 'compromise' solutions reached in their absence, forcefully pushing the line of 'national interest' and 'political realism'. One suspects this scenario exemplifies what is probably passed off as umpire role of the State. Critically viewed, it is not too difficult to see that anxieties of ministers, politicians, political party in power, bureaucrats, police, and security agents intermingle in this mosaic of shifting self-interests and consequent accommodation. There is nothing 'neutral' about the role of the State.

---

[24] For the Nigerian scene see Yesufu, T. M., *An Introduction to Industrial Relations in Nigeria*. OUP/NISER, 1962: Ananaba, W., *The Trade Union Movement in Nigeria*, Ethiope, Benin City, 1969: Cohen, R., *Labour and Politics in Nigeria*, Heinemann. 1974. But most comprehensively dealt with by Otobo, D., *Foreign Interests and Nigerian Unions*, Heinemann, Ibadan, 1986

[25] Representing internationally some 50 million workers in 140 countries, its affiliates in Nigeria are Chemical and Non-Metallic Products Senior Staff Association, National Union of Chemical Footwear Rubber Leather and Non Metallic Products Employees (NUCFRLANMPE), National Union of Electricity Employees, National Union of Petroleum & Natural Gas Workers - NUPENG National Union of Textile, Garment & Tailoring Workers – NUTGTW, Petroleum & Natural Gas Senior Staff Association – PENGASSAN, and Steel and Engineering Workers Union of Nigeria - SEWUN

Employers that resist such settlements find their establishments plagued by more strikes and demands for deportation of expatriate management staff, and with much disgust over 'inconsistency' of government's position, capitulate and effect changes in wages or fringe benefits as was the case in Nigeria over Adebo awards in 1971.[26] Those 'parliamentary' bodies postulated by Dahrendorf (1959) and others conspicuously fail in their assigned tasks, partially succeeded in achieving the more limited objective of *clarifying* issues. In this regard, most disputes and grievance procedures and mediation, conciliation and arbitration facilities are designed to have a *'cooling effect'*, not resolve fundamental conflicts in industry and which, at any rate, they cannot achieve by their very nature or constitution: ultimate power lies elsewhere, in the state, and remorselessly applied to main actors in industry as dictated by circumstances and in line with perceived interests of State elites. One could also reasonably argue that 'hierarchy of workers (non-managerial), their organizations and spokespersons bear the brunt of state coercive powers, making it difficult to achieve this 'compatibility of ideologies' as advocated by Dunlop (1958).

Understanding organization of Farms in the Bush

There seem to be several reasons why a rethink of "received" theories in industrial relations is long overdue. For one, both developmental effort and industrialization processes have become quite politicised, greatly affecting 'roles' played by companies, employers, governments and workers. The survival of multinationals is a major preoccupation of North American and European governments, just as such companies have become active instruments in achieving certain foreign policy or strategic objectives. To this extent, African governments' domestic policies and activism of labour movements receive considerable degree of attention from several quarters, counter-pressures that possess grave distorting effects on policies and institutions alike. This may be regarded as prime cause of crises of social institutions where logically-derived

---

[26] Details in Peace, A., Industrial Protest in Nigeria in Kadt De E. & Williams, G.P. (eds.), *Sociology and Development*, Tavistock. London. 1974.

structures, such as parliamentary negotiating bodies in industry, are foci of social interaction and are yet substantially undermined by external pressures or developments.

At the micro level, plant level, there would be little disagreements over causes of industrial conflict: wages, other conditions of employment, discipline, violation of agreements, grading, training and promotion, hours of work, discrimination, union structure and management style and tactics. And as has clearly been shown, the general distribution of power in society, foreign and/or intelligence intrigues, government's policies, actual conduct of politicians and public officials, and income distribution also contribute to influencing nature of workers' demands, course of industrial conflict and bargaining context itself.

For another, trade unions in these areas, in several significant respects, function differently and are hardly social welfare bodies European workers were used to in those heady times of their development: in many areas and quite often ethnic associations have historically assumed such functions in colonial Africa.[27] Unions could then be said to have whittled down their functions, specializing in the fight for higher wages and betterment of other general conditions of employment, and this they have in common with trade unions in all economies. This does not require extrapolations from European experiences which are inevitably culture-bound in crucial respects. Organizational formats may be emulated, for the sake of argument but not the transfer of cultural traits, norms and historical experiences: thus seemingly familiar institutions would function differently in dissimilar cultural contexts; indeed, differences between American and British or French trade unionism are astonishing despite sharing racial origin and certain historical experiences (cf. Australia and New Zealand).

Similarly the fetish of 'collective bargaining' must not be overdone. It is a situational and logical response to specific economic and political sets of conditions; the absolute necessity for each party to meet its survival objectives. It may also be observed that:

---

[27] See Little. K., *West African Urbanization*, Cambridge University Press. 1965: Wallerstein, I., Voluntary Associations' in Coleman, J.S. Rosberg, C. G. (eds.), *Political Parties and National Integration in Tropical Africa, op. cit.*

a) empirically, collective bargaining, however defined, has always been confined to few Nigerian or African establishments and as such issues covered and instituted grievance and disputes procedures may not be regarded as representative of all industrial sectors;

b) that statutory regulation of terms of employment has become dominant mode, replacing in some sectors and generally setting the stage for truncated form of collective bargaining in such workplaces; and

c) from a) above, the overwhelming majority of working persons, concentrated in what has been labelled "informal sector" are exposed to undiluted powers of employers.

What these three observations have in common and appears insufficiently stressed is that collective bargaining is a *power relationship*. If management draws legitimacy from 'custom and practice', acceptance of institution of private ownership of means of production, and correctness of its position in relation to state laws and regulations, this leaves little room for 'bargaining' and what such activity usually conjures. This reality suggests compromises are either forced by tactics of workers or conceded on some recognition of self-interest, the possibility of disorder, change in power relationships, and maintenance of network of relationship prevailing among and between leaders of all the parties. Some would say a combination of these possibilities but the nature of some compromises, which go against both state regulations and what management had previously defined to be 'taboo', seem to suggest that initial resort to formalistic positions in conflict situations indicates a reluctance to confront issues headlong, or a ploy to undercut and test will of other parties.

It also indicates that frontiers of agreements are constantly shifting in response to numerous variables, including negative sanctions as contained in state regulation and power and "revolutionary potential" of workers. This may not be particularly obvious in daily developments within individual enterprises but as conflict simultaneously occurs in several establishments and escalates, the State apparatus swings into action, with opening salvoes coming from prominent politicians or legislators echoing now familiar slogans of 'threats to public interests' and 'national security' especially when workers in the oil and gas and energy sectors lead such protests or downing of tools as it were.

I think it immensely realistic to say the nature of industrial conflict is therefore problematic. The formal distinction between 'economic' and 'political' strikes, as has been clumsily distinguished in forms of "disputes of rights" and "dispute of interests" in the Nigerian Trade Dispute Act, is hardly illuminating. First, interests often transform into rights over time. Second, the economic and political, however defined separately, remain inseparable in practice; too many businessmen are politicians, too many companies fund political campaigns, too many bureaucrats, members of judiciary and military own shares in companies, and the fact of employment and unionism organized in and around significant privately-owned companies means that government would unlikely formulate policies that might hasten their collapse or disinvest in a hurry. Thus a significant conflict situation in several industries would tend to dissolve this binary distinction.

It is also to be noted that industrial conflict is not all of the time predicated on workers objections to certain practices or new policies. As Dahrendorf pointedly put it, the whole superordination-subordination edifice in industry is perpetually conflict-generating: the act of 'managing' people is a power relationship and conflictual. The crises of social institutions have plainly been wrought by the difficult and increasingly delusory task of equating authoritarian organization of production for private benefit with the general good.

Dynamics of Overseer and Other Species in the Bush

Before we comment on the likely directions of State embeddedness in industrial relations in Nigeria, a recapitulation of why and how it had been intimately embroiled might prove useful, if only to distil the essentials of what has so far been said in this Lecture. Some of the reasons for this Yesufu (1984, 33) has, most fortunately for us, conveniently grouped under four broad categories of economic, historical and international imperatives, its status as the dominant employer, and political and social. A brief comment on some of the arguments provided by Yesufu and subsumed under the above headings is in order, not because the classification itself is defective but because he has imputed certain 'intentions' of the State and made some assertions about industrial relations practices which require a critical second look. Some do, indeed, seem difficult to sustain both historically and empirically. More important, Yesufu has consistently presented one of the most influential and sophisticated analyses of industrial relations processes in Nigeria and should rightly earn more attention.

Under the group of 'economic' reasons, Yesufu (1984, 33) observes that 'the State acquires a vested interest in the industrialization process, the success of which…depends to an incalculable extent upon the skills, attitudes and efficiency of the industrial labour force and it relations with management.' Furthermore, that 'industrial strife even in one major enterprise or industry could cause economic chaos or stagnation through linkage effects. In these circumstances, governments feel the compulsion to be specially concerned with industrial relations, because of the extent to which these relations determine the levels of productivity and the effective utilization of scarce capital and other resources.'

The issue raised here goes beyond our immediate interest and the confines of industrial relations proper, having more to do with development strategies. However, in relation to what I may label the "political economy" of industrial relations, it may be that rapid expansion in public investments has sharpened the manipulative instincts of those public servants who manage these portfolios for greater returns. This may explain their interest in the restive nature of organized labour and in the latter's attempts to resist offers of 'special inducements' to foreign financial sources and technical partners as indicated by Yesufu himself. If so, it has to be said that large-scale investments by the State only recently (i.e. in the 1970s), became a feature of the situation and can hardly account for the deep involvement of the State in industrial affairs throughout much of our earlier history. Secondly, much of the 'general economic chaos or stagnation through linkage effects' referred to appear directly attributable to the nature of the capitalist system (local and international) itself (cyclical 'booms' and 'depressions') and the "dependent" nature of the Nigerian economy with its highly inflated and expensive 'development projects'. The irrelevance of some of these 'white elephants' to meaningful national development, brazen official corruption and the general mismanagement by State elites of 'scarce capital and other resources' form another element of the situation. These, unfortunately, do not vitiate Yesufu's second point; governmental fear of the possibility of industrial strife resulting in chaos. But such a fear can only be in relation to the conduct of, and the social and economic policies adopted by government and State elites themselves. The greater such fears, the more ineffective and bankrupt such policies are. This aside, rivalry between State elites and within the political class itself has contributed in no small way to the very odd geographical siting or location of these 'projects', often against the recommendations of consultants and experts as contained in feasibility reports. This has not only escalated costs but also created all manner of problems for respective labour forces which are sometimes forced to work in areas devoid of housing, water, food, and facilities of any kind, much like building a settlement from scratch. Such workers, understandably, ask for somewhat different terms or allowances from other public employees, differentials which 'government' refuses to entertain, thus leading to strikes, followed by charges or 'economic sabotage' from State functionaries, detentions and summary dismissals.

The consolation perhaps is that it has never been contended that three General Strikes since 1945 (i.e. as at 1978) and an untold number of strikes in both public and private establishments have led to 'general economic chaos or stagnation through linkage effects'. This 'fear' of government and of State elites should, perhaps, be more appropriately seen as part and parcel of rationalizing and 'selling' to all concerned an essentially anti-labour policy, and to reflect the composition of the State rather than an objective assessment of the situation on the ground.

Under 'historical and international imperatives', Yesufu has drawn attention to those pressures, whether political, moral or otherwise, brought to bear by reformers, politicians, metropolitan governments, on colonial administrations and post-colonial governments to fulfil certain international obligations, whether to the United Nations (or League of Nations before it) or to conventions of the International Labour Office (now Organization), in so far as they relate to labour or industrial relations 'actors'. Such pressures have served as an impetus for State intervention in the form of specific legislation. We have already noted, in this regard, the resistance of various colonial administrations to passing legislation recognizing the right of workers to organize and form trade unions, and the ultimate prohibition, after considerable pressure from the Colonial Office and protests by communities and conscript labour, of the use of forced labour. These are forms of State intervention. They also include the legal enactment and enforcement of the length of the working day and week, of contracts of employment, legislation on safety and injury at work, and attempts to establish minimum wage rates in 'sweated' trades, some of which were the subject of investigation by the Sofola Commission (1957).

But Yesufu (1984, 33) moves on to very uncertain ground when he claims that 'before Independence the colonial powers in Africa intervened in industrial relations to implement certain labour policies which were developed and tested in their home countries, and which had become an inseparable adjunct of their social and political philosophy and systems of government,' and contends that 'such intervention appears to have been regarded as part of the civilizing mission of the colonial administration.'

Now, aside from low wages which prevailed in industrializing Britain for centuries, it is difficult to find equivalents of these 'well tested' labour policies as applied in the colonies. During centuries of slave trading abroad, for instance, slaves were legally free in Britain itself. In Britain there was no precedent for the use of forced labour more recently, nor of compulsory registration of unions. Indeed, even right up to the first decade of the twentieth century when employment of children and women was rampant in Britain, the United States of America and the rest of Europe, only able-bodied men were forcibly recruited in Nigeria although legislation was later to be passed prohibiting this method of recruitment.

It may be that Yesufu has in mind other institutional arrangements and legislation such as the Whitley Councils and Trade Union Ordinances. Whitley Councils themselves were not introduced in Britain till 1917 and, as Arthur Marsh, OBE, has pointed out to me in one of his several comments on an earlier essay, joint machinery for negotiation and participation was widely developed in Britain during the First World War of 1914-18, but when formally advocated by government 'after the war, found employers unwilling to share control with their employees.'[28] Such Councils were introduced into Nigeria's public sector about thirty years later with equally dismal results. The 1938 Trade Union Ordinance has been claimed to have been modelled along the lines of the United Kingdom Trade Unions Act of 1871 but, as already indicated, its crucial provisions on compulsory registration (and legal and other consequences of de-registration), compulsory yearly returns, and the categories of persons who could hold union jobs, were not contained in the 'parent' Act. The only common denominator was 'voluntary' recognition of unions by private employers with both parties committed to collective bargaining. The latter, as earlier discussed, was rendered largely ineffectual by the 1941 Trade Disputes (Arbitration & Inquiry) Ordinance, the authoritarian and undemocratic nature of colonial political order, the Nigerian General Defence Regulations which institutionalized forced labour, not to speak of the liberal use of police and soldiers on protesting workers and communities and to provide coercive support for rationing and a crude incomes policy. The point, of course, is that the 1938 Nigerian Trade Union Ordinance is a far cry from the British Act, both in content and intent, and operated differently and under different cultural, political and social circumstances.

On the 'civilizing mission' argument of Yesufu (1984), I am hardly persuaded to think he actually believed colonial officials were on a civilising mission. It was pretty much established that most colonial officials, staff of the Colonial Office, and spokesmen of British business circles were largely aware of the reprehensive nature both of forced labour and the brutal killings of striking workers and of protesting members of various communities and other unwholesome aspects of colonial 'labour policy'. The 'civilizing mission' presentation was directed at minimizing the outrage felt by the British public at large and reformist groups in particular, notwithstanding how the anti-unionism of colonial employers was often disguised by statements claiming either 'over-sophistication' of unionism *per se* or the 'primitivism' of colonized

---

[28] Marsh, A. I., OBE, Former Director of Industrial Relations Unit, St. Edmund Hall, University of Oxford. He has published extensively and is the author of several books including the *Concise Encyclopaedia of Industrial Relations*, Gower, 1977. He supervised my doctoral thesis.

workers struggling to develop their own forms and concepts of trade unionism in African conditions. There is thus little to support the conclusion that colonial labour policy was in the main used as an instrument for civilizing the 'native', an exercise missionaries thought they were doing rather well at through the spread of formal Western education and religious teachings. The economic advantages for colonial employers and metropolitan industry were clear. The potentially frightening political repercussions within the colony forced substantial modification of 'labour policy', particularly in the 1940s and 1950s. Following this argument, Lord Passfield, specifically cited by Yesufu (1984, 33) and under whose secretaryship of the Colonial Office a flurry of despatches suffused with the civilizing mission syndrome are supposed to have appeared, was, undeniably a reformer and an astute political animal. He was, perhaps, more preoccupied with the provision of political 'safety valves' in the colonies and preventing colonial trade unions and other protest movements from falling into 'wrong' hands than with any civilizing mission. This is not to deny the presence of racialists and the occurrence of racism. Some colonial officials pursued racism single-mindedly and encouraged official resistance to much-needed changes in this regard (Nicholson, 1969).

More surprisingly, Yesufu (1984, 33-34) has precious little to say about the consequences for all parties and the general tenor and drift of industrial relations of the policies adopted by relevant State authorities as the major employer. He does mention that the State's example 'becomes the standard for the regulation of employer and employee relations in other sectors of the economy', but fails to examine the said 'example', an exercise that might have thrown more light on the role of the State in industrial relations in Nigeria. Instead, he takes off at a tangent with a broad criticism of trade unions: 'Thus, the nascent trade unions, because of their inability seriously to negotiate with employers, tend generally to adopt the apparently easier but, perhaps, more compelling political strategy and battle cry for their employers to conform with government wage rates, labour standards and conditions of employment' (p. 34). Yesufu seems not to approve of the tendency of trade unions and their members to compel private employers, by declaring trade disputes and embarking on strikes, to conform with 'government wage rates, labour standards and conditions of employment'. Implicit in this position is that these government wage rates, labour standards and conditions of employment are either in themselves to be condemned or, that they are not in the interest of private employers who would seek to keep down labour and other operational costs in the quest for higher profits. Although some of these concerns are not the immediate focus of this Lecture, it may be observed in passing that the labour standards and conditions of employment prevailing in most of the private (the handful of medium and large companies probably account for over seventy per cent of employed hands in this sector) were between 1902 the early 1970s superior to those of the public sector! The pertinent question, from the private employer's point of view, might be what the ultimate objective of the numerous wages and salaries tribunals was in establishing minimum wage rates for low paid employees along with a basic floor of non-wage (fringe) benefits (transport and rent allowance and so forth) - equalisation or further increases in wages and fringe benefits on offer by them? Ubeku (1983, 105), who incidentally was the president of NECA and former managing director of Guinness Nigeria Limited, categorically states that 'for years the Association (NECA, formed in 1957) fought to prevent the introduction of a housing allowance and transport allowance for workers.' The ways of achieving these ends would of necessity admit of conflicting views because of partisanship and self-interest. This is precisely why such policies as adopted by the State as the largest employer of labour, underlying considerations and philosophy, and their implications for workers and private employers should have been thoroughly examined by Yesufu.

A final observation on this account is that the Nigerian State and private employers are as 'nascent' as trade unions. If umbrage is taken against the *modus operandi* of the trade unions which Yesufu has seen in terms of 'nascency' and an 'inability seriously to negotiate with employers' with a consequent 'compelling political strategy', he is taking us back to the so-called Kilby/Weeks debate of the late 1960s which, in the main, sought to establish the primacy of 'political' as against 'economic' factors in the wage bargain situation in Nigeria.[29] I have since pointed out that the distinction between 'economic' and 'political' in bargaining relationships remains at best dubious, whether within the enterprise, the industry or nationwide, both remain inseparable in practice.[30] For much of the history of industrial relations in Nigeria, the matter for concern since colonial times, as we now know, has been the employers' reluctance seriously to negotiate unless compelled by circumstances generated by workers, the State, or increased competition in the product market, rather than the incapacity or unwillingness of the unions to negotiate.

Concerning the last group of factors Yesufu (1984, 34) labelled 'political and social', he pertinently observes that 'poor industrial relations', including strikes, which lower or suspend production, cut into incomes and welfare of workers and their dependents, will generally affect the conditions of work and life of a substantial section of the population.' His more illuminating observation, to my mind, is on the nature of the salaried and wage-earning populations which, he has rightly noted, 'constitutes (particularly in developing countries) the best educated, the most articulate, highly organized and vocal elements in society, who therefore wield tremendous political influence, not only in urban areas where they reside, but also in villages.' We may note in this regard that:

a) an overwhelming majority of the salaried and wage-earning population is employed by the State;

b) preferences and rivalries of the salaried and wage-earning population also influence the character and composition of the State;

c) such power and influence as they wield within the State system is used in challenging the counter-claims of those in the private sector, either as members of management or shareholders of a sort; and

d) industrial relations policies therefore simultaneously project certain sectional interests and attempts at reconciling conflicting interests,

---

[29] Kilby, P., 'Wage Determination in Nigeria: Failure of the Anglo-Saxon Model,' *op. cit.*; and John Weeks' replies in *Journal of Developing Areas*, 5 (2), 1971

[30] See my 'Bureaucratic Elites and Public Sector Wage Bargaining in Nigeria,' *Journal of Modern African Studies*, 24 (1), 1986

outcomes largely dependent on the constellation of forces mobilised by contending groups and issues at stake.

The two 'political and social' reasons adduced by Yesufu in explaining State "intervention" in industrial relations are that 'the State, as a guardian of the social conscience and welfare, feels compelled to ensure that working conditions are humane, fair and reasonable' and in the ex-colonial territories, 'the working class was often a strong ally in the nationalist struggle, and the post-Independence governments have accordingly generally felt committed to assuring progressively better conditions of employment for the workers' (1984, 34).

Little comfort can be drawn from the notion of the Nigerian State as 'guardian of the social conscience and welfare', even if successive 'development plans' contained State's intention to create a better tomorrow. In view of our history and the conduct of our elites, one would like to believe that what Yesufu has in mind is what the State *ought* to become. Similarly, if the supposed commitment of post-colonial governments to progressively better conditions of employment for workers derives from the need to compensate the latter for their role in the nationalist struggle, in the Nigerian experience, there may exist the twin problems of faulty diagnosis and insufficient appreciation of historical antecedents. For one thing, very few current politicians and workers were involved in the 'nationalist struggle' and such lingering sentiments and nostalgia are unlikely to be pervasive. The bulk of the people comprising the wage labour force today were only born since the 1970s; most have only read about nationalist struggles. Second, the nationalist struggle itself was only partially an issue of 'self-determination' and termination of alien colonial rule; it was also primarily a struggle and competition among and between various components of indigenous elites for position and privilege within the colonial structure proper, with the workers and their organizations largely relegated to the sidelines and excluded from the spoils and perks of office since the 1950s. There has been little remotely to suggest, from all the political mayhem, arson, thuggery, corruption and suppression of political dissent which characterized immediate post-colonial politics that 'progressively better conditions of employment of workers' could have been a preoccupation of most politicians. The rest of the first decade (1966-70) was taken up by more heart-rending social crises, culminating in a civil war. Water of sorts has undoubtedly passed under the undeniably shaky bridge since 1970 and a consensus is by no means assured over: a) whether there has been an improvement, relative to inflation and standards of living, in conditions of employment, and b) whether any observable improvements enjoyed by a limited number of wage earners (managerial groups in particular) have been due to direct government policy or worker activity, or business profitability. If the intention to improve the general conditions of workers has been existing, this has been amazingly been at variance with the process whereby each concession has been achieved by organized labour at considerable personal cost and conflict and against the opposition of employers and the political class. Not even in the old Soviet Union, China under Mao, and Cuba, communist countries, is 'government' commitment to progressively better conditions of employment for workers assured; there are always conflicting priorities and interests, mediated only by power relations between classes and groups. This fact alone is reason enough for close scrutiny of proposed and current 'government' policies, particularly in such political environments as prevail in Nigeria, where serious decisions and policies are decided upon with little discussion or consultation and in which regional and ethnic interests appear to loom very large. What the 'national interest' is therefore remains perpetually problematic no matter how strongly the observer believes in the right of government to legislate and make laws.

The Overseer and the Bush

In the context of what has loosely been labelled "an underdeveloped capitalist economy", the logic governing the involvement of the State in industrial relations is, as aptly summed by Yesufu (1984, 34), 'rooted in economic, social and political foundations and has both national and international dimensions.' On the whole, repressive governments care very little about such 'international dimensions' and even countries like the United States of America, Britain and most European Union group of countries which loudly proclaim their democratic virtues, have found reasons not to ratify various conventions and recommendations of the

ILO and resolutions of the UNO, while sustaining dictatorships in Asia, South America and Africa. There are other important aspects which surprisingly did not catch Yesufu's attention as they remain crucial to any meaningful discussion of both politics and role of the State in "underdeveloped" economies.

One such missing international dimension is the position of the Nigerian economy in the 'world economy' or "world capitalist system".[31] Whether as a producer of certain minerals in demand or as a consuming unit, the economic relations of Nigeria are predominantly and firmly with Western countries. Hence on strategic (military), economic and ideological grounds, the maintenance of 'political stability', the safety of 'foreign investments', and the availability of institutional avenues for transferring profits abroad remain important goals for which the affected Western countries, particularly the United States of America, Japan, Germany, Britain and France, would do much to achieve. Likely 'threats' to these goals could come from: a) the elites (political, economic, cultural, etc.); and b) organized labour and the peasantry.

From all that has been said so far, bearing in mind the fusion of politics and business, widespread official corruption, the extensive personal economic interests of powerful factions of elites of the State system, the dependence of indigenous economic elites on subsidiaries of multinational companies and on Western financial institutions, the relative absence of revolutionary intellectual activity, the general predatory activities and disposition of this class of Nigerians, it seems doubtful whether any serious threat could possibly emanate from the elites, excepting their incompetence rendering the country ungovernable. The profits remitted abroad by subsidiaries of multinational companies would compare favourably with the amounts siphoned out by various factions of the elites.[32] But there remains that possibility, that very remote chance by my reckoning, identified by Andre Gunder Frank (1969) in respect of certain regimes in nineteenth century Latin America,

---

[31] See Wallerstein, I., *World System Analysis: An Introduction*, Duke University Press, Durham and London, 2004.

[32] Part of the profits 'earned' by subsidiaries of multinational companies actually go to some members of the elite, and are usually built into the highly inflated costs of projects, as commissions, or as outright bribes in many cases.

that 'nationalist' political classes could develop independent and self-generating economies to replace dependence on primary production and dependence on the import of a wide range of consumer items. In the case of Nigeria, the post-Civil War indigenization drive that might have been a 'patriotic' and 'nationalistic' act if it had been carefully implemented turned out, as earlier noted, to have the rather limited objective of creating a small indigenous business group which still fronted for foreign investors, increasing the number of elites in nominal managerial positions, and opening up positions of authority for competing State elites in a much-expanded public sector. Nor could the more recent military interventions into politics and successive coups be represented as shifts in the ideological positions of the political elite. Economic development is still largely seen in terms of an 'import-substitution strategy', 'transfer of technology' in the forms of assembly plants and 'industries' that require imported 'raw materials'. Presumably, as it is officially argued in late 1970s till mid-1980s, more prudent management of scarce foreign exchange by adopting a 'fairer' system of allocating import licences and foreign exchange among 'genuine' importers and 'respectable' companies might get better results. Deregulation and privatisation of sorts, since the 1990s, is yet to provide remedy to challenges of earning and managing foreign exchange and "growing" the economy to lift aggregate incomes and standards of living in any modest, let alone dramatic, fashion.

This leaves organized labour and the peasantry as the more likely threats to private profits and foreign investments. The political elite itself would induce these threats by its consistent show of an embarrassing capacity to generate political instability by its own clumsiness and general incompetence at resolving internal contradictions and rivalries—consequently jeopardizing the *status quo* itself. The activities of organized labour and of peasantry need have no original intention to restrict private profits and throw out foreign investments, for this suggests to an inherent revolutionary quality to their activities which is not necessarily the case.

However, both intended and unintended radical repercussions appear from protests and other activities of these classes of Nigerians. These include the continuous impoverishment of rural populations as a result of largely urban-centred 'development' policies, an almost suicidal neglect of agriculture in preference to 'industrialization' (a misnomer and euphemism for indiscriminate importation of consumer goods and assembling of an assortment of electronic goods and of motor vehicles), the general mismanagement of the economy as urban populations have great difficulty in making ends meet as a result of inflation and scarcity of imported food items (most ironically and tragically dubbed 'essential commodities'), and the demonstration effect of conspicuous consumption and life-styles of the elites and of open abuse of office and official corruption.

Thus more than ever before, the wage-earning population, peasant farmers and the mass of the unemployed and urban poor have begun to relate their worsening economic plight directly to the woeful failure and inadequacies of government economic and social policies and operations, or to the activities of 'middlemen' and the business community in general. The latter includes the trading subsidiaries of multinational companies and the consortia of Western financial institutions which are held to collude with political and bureaucratic elites in 'generating' and financing highly inflated 'contracts' and 'projects' that have only a marginal impact on their marginalized existence. Growing demands for 'better leadership', food, housing, higher wages, social amenities, a more effective distribution system without middlemen, less imports and the abandonment of import licences, the establishment of industries that utilize local raw materials, curtailment of the activities of multinational companies and a greater say in governance and formulation of national policies by representatives of workers, students, peasants, and other groups considered deprived in this process, all portend fairly serious consequences for elites and the *status quo.*

The relevance of all this is shown in the exertion of constant pressure on the State authorities by Western governments, with the intention of influencing various policies, especially those relating to industry and labour. These pressures take various forms, overt or covert, diplomatic, economic and political (withholding of aid, grants, loans, refusal to reschedule debts, etc.) and military pressure in a few instances. The character of elites, and particularly their internal cohesion and vision, substantially determines resistance or acceptance of such routine pressures. Sometimes such pressures may, in the short term, be in the interest of the general population, especially when they result in the overthrow or rejection of a particularly corrupt regime or leadership. But this may also be a rear-guard action on the part of foreign interests and other alarmed factions or sections of the elite in protecting their economic and political investments. In all, it is a dialectical relationship which removes the possibility of a passive role for elites and other groups, thus engendering volatile political conditions and a fragile State.

In attempting to capture, in a single phrase, the role of the Nigerian State in industrial or employment relations, the utmost caution should therefore be exercised in applying such notions or concepts as 'voluntarism'.[33] In this connection Tayo Fashoyin (1980, 92) simply asserts that '...the basic characteristic of the British industrial relations system, i.e., the doctrine of voluntarism, was entrenched in Nigeria's industrial relations...and it is important, therefore, to point out at this initial stage that voluntarism is another term for abstentionism.'[34] Ubeku (1983, 1) makes a similar claim, noting that since Independence and the first military regime, 'Nigeria has moved away from the voluntary ethic in industrial relations into one of government involvement and intervention'. Yesufu (1984, 39) espouses a similar thesis, while Peter Kilby (1967) assumes such a transfer of institutions, norms, etc., to enable him to lament the 'failure' of an Anglo-Saxon model of industrial relations in Nigeria as earlier pointed out.

Some of these writers would seem to have failed to separate official pronouncements, designed, in large measure, to win support while disarming potential critics inside and outside the country, from the actual tactics and methods employed. The very claim that the British system, no matter how vulgarized, was, in the first instance, transplanted in Nigeria is simply misplaced, an *illusion*, and contrary to historical facts, and it is not a question of racial and cultural differences alone; there were also qualitative differences. The proletarianization process in Britain was a

---

[33] For a good discussion of the concept and its relevance to the conduct of industrial relations in Britain and the United States of America see Flanders, A., 'The Tradition of Voluntarism', *British Journal of Industrial Relations* (BJIR), XII (3), Nov. 1974; Rogin, M., 'Voluntarism: The Political Foundation of an Anti-political Doctrine', *Industrial and Labor Relations Review*, July 1962; Fink, G.M., 'The Rejection of Voluntarism', *Industrial and Labour Relations Review*, January 1973

[34] *Industrial Relations in Nigeria*, Longman, 1980

product of an overwhelming industrial and social transformation which marked the crucial watershed in the transition of a feudal society into a capitalist one. In Colonial Nigeria, by contrast and from which most Western historiographers routinely take as starting-point of their narratives, the economic activities which prevailed were restricted in the main to construction, mining and trading, and involved only a small fraction of the total population. There were no competing dynasties and kings, queens, princes and Christendom who nominally owned everything, no land-bound serfs, no landless serfs, no artisans (indentured and self-employed), seigniors, mayoralties, the Inquisition and class-ridden and conflict-ridden societies as was typically the case all over what came to be Europe and Britain before the Industrial Revolution. Less than eighty years ago, Major Orde Brown noted in this regard that he had 'been somewhat surprised to find that the situation in Nigeria differs in one respect from that of most African countries, with certain exceptions there are few clearly defined areas where large numbers of men are regularly employed (1941, 67).'[35] The only common denominator in both situations was the existence of conditions permitting the creation of wage labour, the responsible factors differing in type, scope, time, space and role, as their results have been starkly different too. Historical experiences can hardly be recreated within the same cultural area in a different time period in view of differential inter-generational socialization, technical advancements and social change, not to speak of transfer to totally different continents and races. This is, indeed, why British industrial relations, institutions, processes and practices have not been transferred to the United States of America, Canada, New Zealand and Australia, countries which were at one-time British colonies and whose controlling segments of their populations even share a common racial stock as mentioned earlier.

In the light of colonial realities in Nigeria, with colonial governors, residents and other officials combining judicial and political functions, and the intimate involvement of the State in the 'recruitment', 'motivation' and 'disciplining' of the labour force, Fashoyin's equating of 'voluntarism' in the Nigerian context with the supposed 'abstention' of

---

[35] Orde-Brown, G. M., *Labour Conditions in West Africa*, HMSO, Cmd, 6227, 1941.

the State from industrial relations is a most baffling illusion.[36] His claim of a move away from voluntarism to greater intervention is also an illusion, a gross misrepresentation of the process of formalizing constant State involvement. Subsequent legislation since the 1938 Trade Unions Ordinance represents an attempt to codify the bases of action and the activities of various State agencies and colonial officials, a formerly personalized system that had gone awry and become obsolete and could no longer withstand the passions, pressures and ideas of more recent years. A fragmented political authority system had become increasingly centralized, pockets of intense economic activities have broadened into a national economy, concomitantly creating a national labour market and labour movement. A situation of two or more major private employers has given way to variety and larger numbers, including subsidiaries of multinational companies. In short, the crude colonial economy had progressively been overtaken by a more rationalized, albeit "dependent" capitalist system, boasting more sophisticated 'sets of actors' who now operate at the national level and make demands on the total system. Thus relations have become more contractual in response. *At no period, then or now, has State involvement in industrial relations been less. It has certainly never been absent by definition.*

Employers and employees do enjoy a measure of autonomy in settling internal problems within their establishments without the immediate intervention of the law courts and the State. If this is what *voluntarism* is taken to mean, by many of these writers, in the Nigerian context, then there is hardly anything peculiarly British or Anglo-Saxon about it, because such autonomy necessarily prevails wherever the rights of private ownership of property and the means of production are accepted, even perfunctorily. But by no stretch of the imagination can such autonomy be taken to mean the *abstention* of the State from industrial affairs.

There has been no great erosion of the voluntary principle in recent times. Despite a flourish of legislation to govern the conduct of the parties in industrial relations, managements have been able to manage their private empires, collective bargaining has only been marginally affected by growing attempts to establish minimum wages rates and a

---

[36] *Industrial Relations in Nigeria, op. cit.*

basic floor of non-wage (fringe) benefits for lowly paid workers in both the public and private sectors of the economy. It is too easily forgotten that minimum wage legislation and other relevant industrial relations policies only apply to establishments of fifty employees and more, an overwhelming majority of employers thus remain unaffected and able unilaterally to determine terms and conditions of employment, subject only to limited checks imposed by aggrieved workers in the form of demands, rapid personnel turnover or individual acts of sabotage.

The Bush, Climate Change and Final Destination

The Bush

We have arrived at the crossroads of deciding on what to retain or discard from dominant models, clearly recognising obfuscation and falsity wrought by intensive modelling and extensive illusions plaguing most theoretical expositions of private enterprise economy, dynamics of national economies, what companies do and how they are managed to employment relations generally, all which are constituents of the Bush. The largest deceptive canvas is the notion and theory of perfect competition, commonly rendered as a 'free market situation' of many buyers and many sellers amidst free flow of information. There are clearly many distributors, many retailers and many buyers of all sorts of goods and services but only a *few* makers or manufacturers, depending on the good or service in question. The one maker (monopolists) or few makers (oligopolists) dictate prices and other conditions for making their goods or services available, thereby transforming distributors and retailers to status of mere *suppliers* on terms they themselves do not significantly modify. This condition has been labelled "monopoly capitalism" by some (Baran and Sweezy 1966)[37] and asserted to be the norm instead of a "perfect" competition of many buyers and many sellers where the sellers are also the makers/manufacturers/producers, which hardly exists save for certain agricultural produce and even there *a few distributors*

---

[37] Baran, P., *The Political Economy of Growth*, Monthly Review Press, New York, 1957; Baran, P. & Sweezy, P., *Monopoly Capital*, Penguin, Harmondsworth, 1966

constitute themselves into the only supply channels and are usually in a position to influence, if not determine, both farmers' prices and other buyers' or consumers' costs.

As for the "free flow of information", the second leg of the perfect competition theory, even impressive as current levels of information communications technologies are, so-called social media in particular, they have not made this possible, aside from the mode of existence of individuals rendering it impossible to have the time to seek and obtain knowledge of prices of services and goods they routinely consume as offered by all competing retailers. It has in fact been the case of new businesses springing up (as others collapse) to take advantage of and profit from a persistent, chronic information gap, segmenting markets. In this wise, the illiberal use of the label "free market economy" by many social scientists, politicians, national and international development institutions or agencies in the last four decades especially is thus part modelling and part illusory, conflating hypotheticals with reality.

So, intra-continental and inter-continental business opportunities and interests give birth to multinational or transnational companies, with subsidiaries located in all continents. Multinational companies and other investors compete for global markets and global sources of raw materials, with strategies fashioned to cope with or adapt to local circumstances of national economies. This, in turn, has given birth to conception of a *global economy* and of an *international economic system*. The global economy is said to comprise national economies, regional and sub-regional economic groupings (e.g. ECOWAS), regional and sub-regional financial and trade regulating institutions (e.g. African Development Bank), international trade, financial and development institutions/agencies, relevant United Nations trade and financial agencies, and transnational/multinational companies. And the structure of the global economy may be roughly differentiated along the following lines or classification: a) long-industrialised economies; b) newly industrialising economies; c) raw materials-producing economies; d) capital-intensive and rich economies, of which only a few of the long-industrialised economies are; and e) poor capital economies. While the *international economic system*, simplified considerable, is how various units which make up the global system go about investing and financing such investments. Typically, the units operate through Stock Exchanges, transnational or multinational companies, and jumping into the foray are the World Bank and the International Monetary Fund, regional and international credit financial institutions and thousands of a variety of fund managers, and insurance companies. As noted earlier, the underlying philosophy or ideology of this international economic system is that of leaving the supply of goods and services and the determination of their prices and other terms to "market forces", demand and supply. The push therefore, since the mid-1980s has ostensibly been for "deregulated markets", whether of exchange rates, finance and financial derivatives, shares and futures, services, or labour, transactions that should exclude involvement of governments or state authorities. Of course, this has substantially been modelling also, and did not even require an openly tariffs-imposing, "protectionist" President Donald Trump in the USA to show consistent regulatory intervention of governments and States and in spite of the activities of the World Trade Organisation (WTO); there are, strictly speaking, no deregulated markets - locally, regionally and internationally. Patents, copyright, other licensing arrangements, trade and distribution and agency agreements basically determine who may be a manufacturer and distributor of tradable goods and services, especially across national boundaries, and by the same logic the structure of the industries and economy as a whole. Each industry is thus dominated by either one company or by a few, and, which in the Nigerian context, serves to define "organised private sector" of major (mostly foreign and subsidiaries of multinational companies) employers and where trade unionism occurs. Organised private sector, institutionally represented by employers' organisations, the Nigeria Employers Consultative Association (NECA), Chambers of Commerce and the Manufacturers Association of Nigeria, includes segments of agriculture, banking and financial services, textile-garment-tailoring, hotel and personal services, construction, telecommunications, petroleum-gas and road transport industries. The rest of the private sector is populated by a handful of distributors and hundreds of thousands of retailers employing fewer hands individually and also explains why the food, beverage and tobacco sector is the least organised, but the largest component of the effervescent "informal sector".

The formation and development of trades unions in the public sector, as may be garnered from previous discussions of these during and after colonisation, followed different trajectories, public sector unions being earlier and all unions' structures following closely those of employers, that is departments, agencies and ministries at the centre, regional, state and local government levels, and respective branches of companies. These were partially "rationalised" in the 1977-1978 government-led reorganisation exercise that produced separate forty-three 'industrial' unions for 'junior' workers and fifteen (check) 'senior staff associations' for 'senior' workers respectively, with industrial unions compulsorily affiliated to one central labour organisation, the Nigerian Labour Congress (NLC), and nine employers organisations. The Abacha regime supervised the reduction of industrial unions to some twenty-nine. On 20 March 2005, President Obasanjo amended the Trades Union Act to enable the formal registration of the Trades Union Congress (TUC) as a central labour organisation on 8 August 2005 to which senior staff associations could affiliate.

So what has been the nature of trade unionism in Nigeria more recently? Whatever it is workers do have more popularly been labelled "struggles", broadly at two levels of *micro* and *macro*, the former representing the gist of labour-management relations within individual enterprises and the latter capturing industry-wide, economy-wide, national and international dimensions. It may be pointed out, however, that at the micro level there is a bifurcation of a sort, the 'struggles' of overwhelming number of Nigerian workers and who are in the 'unorganised' sector, both public and private, remain largely undocumented, while, on the other, most narratives ending up as of those in 'organised private sector' where relatively fewer number of workers have managed to form trades unions.

The structure and distribution of public and private employers have obviously been a constraining factor, counteracting moves on workers and trades unions' partly being a major part of struggles at micro and macro levels, also instigating intra-union and inter-union disputes over the decades. The intra-union disputes arise from factional in-fighting while the latter from jurisdictional problems associated with untidy trade union structure. Though occurring infrequently, reliable statistics do not exist as, in any case, most go unreported save where members get drawn in and themselves embark upon sympathy strikes in favour of one or other set of union leaders. The two most prominent cases have been those factions among dockworkers and maritime workers where antagonistic and rival union executives coexisted for years. The intricacies of these situations are better understood in the context of the trade union structure and managements' anti-union and divide-and-rule strategy.

Concerning the structure of the new unions (whether in 1977 or 1997), the label 'industrial union' hardly imparts any true meaning of the situation because of the rather loose usage of the term 'industry' in the Nigerian economy, plus the fact that even by standards of such less rigorous usage unions do straddle several industries. The standard definition of an industrial union has been given as "a trade union whose membership is organized on the basis of representing all grades of workers in a particular industry, and hence includes unskilled, semi-skilled, skilled and sometimes non-manual employee."[38] In its historical usage, as can be seen from the definition, industrial unions only rarely include 'non-manual workers' among their membership, and it would seem in the case of the Nigerian Union of Teachers, for example, that 'profession' has been regarded as synonymous with 'industry'. And not all teachers are even members of the NUT as teachers in tertiary institutions (universities, polytechnics, etc.) have their own unions, the perking order suggesting university teachers might be the 'senior staff' while all other categories of teachers are 'junior workers'!

Furthermore, it has remained unclear how the Administrator of Trade Union Affairs and his team (1976-1977) and other joint committees established for the same purpose over the years managed to demarcate boundaries of an 'industry' in the public sector. It is more likely that strong consideration might have been given to existing structure of the bureaucracy itself, including a measure of recognition extended to distribution of skills or functional specialization within individual ministries. This would probably explain why 'technical' workers belong to the erstwhile Civil Service Technical Workers Union

---

[38] Marsh, A. I., *Concise Encyclopaedia of Industrial Relations,* Gower, 1971

and 'clerical' to the former Civil Service Union. This grouping has inexplicably excluded 'clerical' and 'technical' workers who abound in numerous parastatals if skill or job specialization is the only criterion. It is not as if such technical workers are absent from refineries and exploration departments managed by the Nigerian National Petroleum Corporation or might not be found at the erstwhile state-owned Delta Steel Company, Aladja, employees who respectively belong to National Union of Petroleum and Natural Gas Workers and Iron and Steel Workers' Union of Nigeria.

Each industrial union or senior staff association is a federation of many pre-1977 restructured house unions (dubbed 'house' unions because they were formed around the branches or sections of the same company or establishment), criss-crossing several industries (not applicable to public sector unions) held together by an over-arching national executive and following the traditional divide of public and private sector. In most instances, industrial unions are made up of previous house unions but now referred to as 'branches' or 'units', while making allowance for creation of newer branches and units from more recently established industrial and commercial enterprises and a growing number of parastatals at both federal and state levels.

This federal structure would seem to have encapsulated some of the pre-1976 differences among union leaders and 'general secretaries' as house unions affiliated in the past to rival local central bodies and international labour organisations (WFTU, ICFTU, WCL, etc.) are now grouped under one or the other 'industrial union'. Several conclusions might reasonably be drawn from this:

(a) each industrial union has fossilized, as it were, antagonistic factions;
(b) emergent industrial unions would be more democratic because of existence of these ever-watchful vocal groups;
(c) by the same token, internal administration would be a far more difficult and complex process than prevailed under House Unions.

One special type of inter-union dispute is the one involving the NLC and their affiliates, the national industrial unions, and between the TUC and the senior staff associations. Such relationship as exist between executives of industrial unions and of the NLC would seem to be coloured by three not wholly unrelated factors, namely: (a) differential reactions among union leaders to general developments; and (b) financial links. As for residual animosities, differences in personality, conduct, and general outlook have tended over the decades to 'stabilize' among the older and second generation of trade unionists; some prejudices held by the younger and middle level union leadership calcifying into 'world view' as transmitted by the older generation (and influenced by foreign sponsors of international labour organizations to which they had been exposed) who largely groomed the current crop of union leaders. As already indicated, each industrial union contains many house unions which had been affiliated to rival labour centres and as such, internal decision-making process might be plagued by obstructive tactics of some branches, including withholding of membership dues mentioned earlier. This attritive process would in many be a constant reminder of 'ideological' differences of the past, reinforcing present disagreement as relevant official of the NLC could attempt to exploit such differences in the union in order to make life a bit more difficult for a general secretary or president considered 'too hostile' to the NLC leadership.

A subsidiary consequence, and which brings us to the second factor, is a seemingly in-built propensity on the part of various factions of labour leadership to represent contradictory and opposing positions over issues and strategies. Discordant noises have been made over such dissimilar issues as car loans, pensions, abuse of import licences, retrenchments, social welfare schemes, compulsory salary cuts, general economic policy, and state of the national economy, military rule, and return to civil rule, travails of democratic disorder, etc. The prime motive, as it would seem to an impartial observer, appears to be a persistent urge to either upstage or undermine the NLC or TUC leadership, or faction of labour movement thought to back the organization. A better perspective of the situation might be achieved when it is realized that 'leadership of the labour movement' is less than five hundred critical actors if one were to restrict oneself to president, vice-president, general secretary, deputy secretary and treasurer of the industrial unions and senior staff associations, and from among whom officials of the NLC and TUC are elected. A significant number of these same persons are members of various organs of the NLC and TUC, and it would therefore be difficult to argue the case of any industrial union or senior staff association executive being kept in the dark or of imagined 'undemocratic' inclinations of the NLC and TUC leadership.

The state of financial links between unions and the central bodies have naturally been affected by personal rivalries and animosities and fluctuations in union membership on account of seemingly interminable lay-offs, partly due to the depressed state of the economy although there is some evidence to suggest cynical exploitation of the situation by many a company. Out of what could only qualify to be called vindictiveness, there are members which deliberately withhold their contribution to the coffers of the central labour organisations; there is the category of those which fall back on their dues, sometimes owing up to nine months' dues without offering any explanations or apologies; there are unions which pay regularly but are held by central labour organisation's officials to understate their membership so as to reduce their contribution (which comprise the bulk); and there are members which remit their contributions promptly and pay extra as 'levies'.

Some of the union leaders interviewed have sought refuge in the allegation that the central bodies' officials have not held themselves financially accountable to affiliates. In all this would seem a rather lame excuse because National Executive Council (NEC), which manages affairs of the central bodies, has as sitting members presidents and general secretaries of all affiliates. It has proved exceedingly difficult, if not impossible; in practice for the NLC and TUC executive officials to by-pass this body, aside from the fact that the central bodies submit copies of their yearly audited accounts (after approval of the NEC) to the Registrar of Trade Unions. Such charges might more justifiably be thrown at such affiliates themselves, as individual union members are more likely to claim ignorance of what their executive officials are up to.

An instructive source of discord within the ranks of union leadership since the 1960s is income-generation by way of investments, typically in purchase and running of vehicles for commercial purposes (public transportation), and in landed property, triggering factions and in-fighting over charges of corruption and self-enrichment on the part of some union leaders and bureaucrats. Same two issues generated great acrimony during the tenure of Abdulwaheed Omar's as the NLC president (2007-2015), including the allegation that pensioners and others who invested in advertised housing schemes or estates received neither allocation papers nor certificate of occupancy. These and John Odah's loss of his job as NLC's general secretary in unusual circumstances seemed to have set the stage for the NLC's abortive 8-11 February 2015 11th National Delegates Conference that failed to conclude elections of members to its National Advisory Council (NAC). Though the Conference was reconvened in 12-14 March 2015, this was unable to prevent the emergence of a rival faction which held its own "NLC Conference" at Mainland Hotel, Lagos a few days later and despite the intervention of the National Association of Trade Union Veterans (NATUV).

It would no longer seem a problem of reluctance of union members to pay dues (since automatic check-off obviates this despite provision enabling any union member to contract out of such an arrangement) but more of a state of social relations among members of union bureaucracies, including the NLC and TUC. Even so, this is a partial picture that hardly reflects divisive moves and tactics of private employers and of state functionaries alike, some union officials succumbing to all manner of pressures. In other words, one might all too easily exaggerate the degree of prevailing animosity, which in itself is largely a by-product of labour control strategies deployed with devastating effect by the Federal Ministry of Employment, Labour and Productivity, the Presidency and intelligence and security organizations and by powerful subsidiaries of multinational companies. But at the end of the day, union leaders are responsible for the views that they espouse and their choice of strategies and tactics.

Public policies and Micro-Macro-Struggles in the Federal Public Service since 1990

The government formally extended deregulation to collective relations in industry in the 1991 budget speech, although its intention to do so had been apparent since 1988 when the Cabinet Office (now Office of the Presidency) organized a national conference on uniform remuneration in the public sector, the main thrust being the need to deregulate salaries/wages, fringe benefits and general terms of employment therein.

The relevant section of the budget speech says that:

In the public sector, government accepts that the time has come for collective bargaining to take firm root and for wage fixing to reflect varieties and differences in the ability to pay, as between the federal government, state government, local government and the parastatals. The representatives of these various tiers of government will negotiate directly with the appropriate industrial unions at the level of federal, state or local governments and the parastatals, but always bearing in mind the ability to pay and the imperatives of a good remuneration policy. The federal government will cease to issue general circulars with universal applicability with regards to wages, fringe benefits and conditions of employment to all public agencies.

The major casualties of the structural adjustment programme as implemented from 1989 were the wage bargain or collective bargaining institutions for the *public sector*. In a dramatic departure from existing practice and in reaction to protests by organized labour, the federal government in 1989 announced its 'SAP relief package' in the form of increased money value of fringe benefits, without prior consultation with organized labour and state governments, and at the same time by-passing the National Negotiating Councils in so doing. By 1991 the government more or less spelt out its unwillingness to route relevant matters through these institutions.

Such wage bargain institutions in the public sector, particularly the Productivity, Prices and Incomes Board (PPIB) and the National Negotiating Councils I, II and III, were therefore rendered moribund and ineffectual, the government preferring the method of administrative fiat. Either through pre-emptive moves or in reaction to generalized disquiet and pockets of protests alongside adverse press coverage, the government would appoint *ad hoc* inter-ministerial, bilateral and tripartite committees largely to defuse the situation by addressing themselves with much fanfare to particular issues (e.g. the banning and unbanning of the

NLC, demonstrations against removal of petroleum subsidies, the minimum wage).

The deliberate neglect of these institutions by the government can only but encourage the growth of fractionalised bargaining, the further decreasing of the already precarious legitimacy of government officials at tripartite or bilateral discussions (whenever these occur) as they are perceived rightly by workers' and employers' representatives to lack effective mandate since final say glaringly rested with the Presidency, and generate conflicts in interpretations over what is supposed to have been agreed upon and the manner and timing of implementation.

At state level and since 1985 military governors have been invested with powers to directly interfere in collective bargaining processes. Following hard on the heels of wage refunds to junior workers, that the Babangida regime had unilaterally deducted some months earlier, was a decree which was designed to win back what the government seemed to have lost. The States (Special Development Levies) Decree No. 37 of 1986 had as its first clause:

> the Governor of a State shall have power to levy and deduct monies from the salary earnings and wages of any person employed in the public services of State, civil service, judiciary and other government statutory corporations, commissions, authorities or other agencies or group of persons employed in the private sector of the State, or authorize any person appointed by him to deduct from an employee's salary or wages such other levies as may be deemed necessary to furtherance of the development of the State.

It was back-dated and thereby deemed to have come into force on 11 November, 1985. For peace-time collective bargaining, it was an incredible piece of social legislation which was roundly denounced by all sides of industry. Indigenes of many states have been burdened by all sorts of levies, most times in face of a threat to defaulters of exclusion from having access to health facilities, drugs, schools and other welfare facilities.

Deregulation or decentralization of collective bargaining in the public sector

The arguments about deregulation of collective bargaining since the 1991 budget speech and subsequent empirical evidence suggest that the federal government has tended to use deregulation to represent two related phenomena. In the first usage, deregulation is taken to mean *institutional decentralization*. While in the second, deregulation stands for *laissez faire*, the possibility of parties freely negotiating without the intervention of a third party - the essence of collective bargaining as is conventionally understood. On the surface, the *institutional* decentralization of wage bargain structures and the institutionalization of the *freedom* of the parties to negotiate directly with each other should be to everyone's advantage and should cause no problems at all. In practice, however, there seems to be no official intention whatsoever to maximize this freedom to bargain collectively, but rather an underhanded way of reducing both the existing rates of remuneration in cash and kind and of the freedom and capacity of one of the parties, organized labour, to negotiate in any meaningful sense.

Second, and which flows from the first, is that for state and local governments and parastatals to negotiate and fix wages and other fringe benefits on their own, would lead to the existence of different rates of pay, a return to the geographical wage structure of the 1950s. Although the 1988 conference organized by the Cabinet Office had concluded that 'the present unified remuneration in the public sector within the framework of collective bargaining, equal work for equal pay, should be maintained in the interest of the nation,' the practice since then has been for the different tiers to agree their own rates.

Third, the assumption implicit in the phrase *'capacity to pay'*, is that all state government and local government-level organs must by definition be in a *less* advantaged position financially in relation to the federal government and could only therefore pay *less*. If state/local governments and parastatals were to decide to pay higher rates either because of more effective management of resources, or reaching a better understanding with their respective employees who are residents/indigenes in the case of state governments, or more effective resistance on the part of organized labour at the state or local government level, or through lack of conviction over official economic policies themselves and which are then passed off as federal folly, the federal authorities would themselves have to more than match those rates!

Fourth, taking a cue from the third reason, is that the *'capacity to pay'* factor in the public sector requires further explanations. Parastatals are, at least nominally, under certain ministries and their votes or subventions are budgeted for just as the federal, state and local governments base their own budgets on statutory allocations and projected internally-derived revenue. The *recurrent* expenditure includes provision for wages and fringe benefits. Evidence indicates that it is only when extra-budgetary expenditures are engaged in (that is, expenditures not budgeted for such as donations, purchases of combat tank, planes, other military hardware, projects and contracts) and finances mismanaged that wages and allowances remain unpaid, and talks of 'capacity to pay' abound in official circles. An *incapacity* to pay does not, *in principle*, exist; it is contrived.

The "capacity to pay" factor must then be specifically tied to the implementation of *new rates* arrived at through negotiations or by administrative fiat. For, in-between budgets some occasions do arise that lead the federal, state and local governments into unforeseen expenditures, and in which cases there would be some difficulty in meeting such sudden and new financial obligations. The same for national minimum wage, initial implementation stages riddled by dissension and acrimony and true shortage of funds; but subsequent budgets should then accommodate the new rates.

Fifth is the ease with which the state governments and local governments and political parties, in competition and rivalry under democratic politics could fix wages (and withhold them - as happened in one or two southeast states between 1999 and 2004) and other conditions of service on purely political considerations. If such wages are too low, then disputes and conflicts would be confined to such units only, rather than the current situation of making it national in scope and increasing instability of the system.

Sixth, is that the policy would reinforce federal political arrangements in the country for state governments and local governments to take some initiative on labour matters which, by the provisions of all Nigerian constitutions so far, is a federal responsibility. Sections of the constitution have to be amended and other measures put in place, including a review of the revenue allocation formula in favour of State and local governments, to enable them implement legally (and effectively?) the policy of deregulation of collective bargaining.

Petroleum and Gas Industry

The information below is based on data from NUPENG, PENGASSAN and NNPC Head-Office between 2002 and 2013 indicate most strike actions were as a result of: i) Opposition by workers to government's planned privatization of NNPC downstream subsidiaries; ii) Lack of refurbishing facilities and irregularities in the allocation and distribution of petroleum products at Warri refinery; iii) planned privatization of Kaduna refinery by Federal Government; iv) attempt by Federal Government to privatize the Refineries; and v) protesting the sale of 51% equity of the Port Harcourt refinery to Blue Star Consortium by Federal Government. While other causes of protests in the oil and gas industry generally have been:

- lack of central body, i.e. employers' association in each company to negotiate internally hence no standardized system of wage structure/conditions of services;
- casualization of labour;
- outsourcing of jobs;
- non-application of local content policy;
- job losses caused by crisis and 'militant' activities in the Niger delta;
- breach of collective agreement;
- competition and rivalry amongst employers creating instability on terms and conditions of employment within the industry;
- anti-union activities through victimization of union officials;
- management accused of favouring expatriates at the expense of Nigerian workers;

- payment of arbitrary severance pay to discharged employees without negotiations;
- racism, intimidation and harassment of Nigerian workers; and
- unilateral implementation of pension act without consultation with the union.

The officials of the Federal Ministry of Labour and Productivity say that the Ministry does its utmost best to settle dispute(s) brought by parties in this industry at conciliation stage and hardly allows it (them) to proceed to the other stages due to the sensitive nature and strategic importance of the industry to the national economy.

The General Secretary of NUPENG affirms the Ministry's position, citing the case of *NUPENG* v. *Maritime Workers Union* jurisdiction dispute where the maritime union wanted workers in the upstream sector to belong to their union instead of the NUPENG. This and similar cases are resolved by Ministry officials.

Based on the information supplied, there were no wage-related strikes. What may be distilled from the foregoing is that employers in this industry have attractive remuneration packages for employees, more favourable than those prevailing in other industries, including banking and finance. However unilateral decisions, unfair treatment of employees and anti-union activities appear to be factors responsible for disputes amongst others. The communication channel used by government must be flawless and free from distortion in order to forestall misinterpretation and misrepresentation of government's intention by the mass media and the public which could generate uncertainty and crisis, e.g. the tension generated by the rumour of government's proposed relocation of the Petroleum Training Institute (PTI) in Warri to Kaduna.

Education Sector

Education is put on the concurrent legislative list in the 1999 Constitution. This means both the federal and state governments have legislative powers as well as functional in respect of education. Statutorily, the Federal Ministry of Education (FME) is at the apex of the regulation and management of education in the country and to discharge this mandate, the ministry is structured into eight departments and three statutory units. Although the FME has overall responsibility for formulating, harmonizing and coordinating policies and monitoring quality in service delivery in the education sector, the ministry is advised in the discharge of these responsibilities by the National Council on Education (NCE), the highest policy formulation body on educational matters which is composed of the Federal Minister of Education and the State Commissioners for Education (FME, 2005).

The involvement of the federal government is largely at the tertiary level and as such, the federal education sector in Nigeria is made of federal universities (27), federal polytechnics and colleges of technology (32), federal colleges of education (20), federal science and technical colleges and federal government colleges (83) that are funded almost exclusively by the federal government from public resources.

There are regulatory bodies set up by the federal government to ensure minimum standards at the tertiary level. These are the National Universities Commission (NUC), the National Board for Technical Education (NBTE), and the National Commission for Colleges of Education (NCCE). They are parastatals of the Federal Ministry of Education for ensuring effective administrative control of higher education in Nigeria. They plan organize, manage, fund, supervise and monitor provision and development of the tertiary institutions; as may be appropriate to each commission or board. Each parastatal helps to ensure minimum standard and quality among the institutions. They also play the intermediary and advisory roles between the federal government and the institutional authorities (FME, 2005).

Employment relationships within the federal education sector are not different from what obtains in the Nigerian public service. The industrial relations climate has often been characterized by a deliberate push of government in the direction of a unipolar work order in which the feelings of the other parties involved especially workers, are ignored. It would appear that the government has embraced the unitary ideology in industrial relations practice, which does not recognise the plurality of views/interests.

The union-avoidance strategy of government has made it to be reluctant to negotiate with workers' organisations and when this is done grudgingly, such agreements are observed more in the breach. On several occasions, the federal government has consistently refused to behave like a responsible employer of labour: it has refused to fulfil the basic obligations expected of an employer, including paying wages and salaries as and when due, acceptance of dialogue and negotiation as means of creating workplace harmony. And when workers, through their unions, summon enough courage to confront the government and demand the payment of their legitimate entitlements, government resort to claiming sovereignty. The resultant effect is the prevalence of a turbulent industrial relations climate in the last three decades especially. In the words of the Nigeria Labour Congress, "the relationship with government has not been too cordial while the tendency is for government to see NLC as an adversary."

To represent and advance the interests of employees in the education sector are the Academic Staff Union of Nigeria Universities (ASUU), Non-Academic Staff Union of Universities and Allied Institutions (NASU), Senior Staff Association of Nigerian Universities (SSANU), Academic Staff Union of Polytechnics (ASUP) and Colleges of Education Academic Staff Union (COEASU) and the Senior Staff Association of Universities, Teaching Hospitals, Research and Allied Institutions (SSAUTHRAI). These unions articulate the collective grievances of their members as well as act as their bargaining agents during negotiations.

Within the employment relationship, conflict can be regarded as the difference or divergence of opinions, attitude, disposition and view on a particular issue. Given the antagonistic positions of both management and workers, there are many of such instances of conflict. Over the years, the education sector in Nigeria has become a veritable theatre of conflicts rather than an effective engine for quality human capital development. In actual fact, the past three decades have witnessed quite a number of conflicts caused by factors that are both internal and external to the sector. It should be noted that conflicts have been more prevalent at the tertiary level of the education sector. Teachers in the federal government colleges are regarded as core civil servants who, more often than not, are not favourably disposed towards union activism. It was only around 2004 that they embarked on a fairly long strike action to protest the decision of the federal government to privatise the schools.

The unending conflicts within the federal tertiary education sector have revolved around three major issues; i) funding; ii) improved conditions of service; and iii) university autonomy/academic freedom. These issues have become particularly problematic since the 1980s when structural economic problems and the imposition of neo-liberal economic policies among other factors, have constrained the ability of the federal government to live up to its proprietorial responsibilities. The Academic Staff Union of Nigerian Universities (ASUU) has been frontally involved in addressing the conflict-inducing issues. The other unions have mostly taken a cue from ASUU struggles to make demands of their own, some of which bother on the ridiculous. A good example is the demand for pay parity with academic staff of universities by their non-academic counterparts. Since about the early 1970s, the union of university teachers has had cause to engage government in addressing some of the problems besetting the university system in particular and tertiary education in general. Not unexpectedly, many of these conflicts have resulted in strike actions which became preponderant since the early 1990s.

From the immediate above, there are hardly any of the strike actions that did not involve wage-related issues. But, on many occasions after securing concessions on wage issues, ASUU still insisted on government addressing the other issues before calling off their actions. This, however, cannot be said of the other unions who seem to await ASUU securing agreements with government before making substantially similar demands.

Dispute-settlement mechanism, assessment and suggestions for improvement

Given the inherent contradictions in employment relations, the possibility of eliminating conflicts is very remote. What obtains in reality is an attempt to contain and manage conflicts through a number of regulatory measures. This is meant to minimize what is considered the damaging consequences of conflicts. Industrial relations inherently involve the settlement of industrial disputes through negotiations between workers' representatives and employers. The collective bargaining machinery is one of the institutional mechanisms for the management of conflict. Even though the causes of conflict remain inherent in the structure of social and economic relations, a network of procedures are supposed to contain its expression. Thus, it becomes easy to suppress the more "destructive" manifestation of conflict of the sort Ralf Dahrendorf (1969) has in mind.

The framework for negotiation within the Nigerian public service is institutionally through the National Public Service Negotiating Councils I-III. The Councils, which were recommended by the Udoji Public Service Review Commission (1972-74), cater for the following groups of workers:

(1) Council I- Association of Senior Civil Servants of Nigeria.
(2) Council II
    (a) Nigeria Civil Service Union (which caters for intermediate and junior non-technical grades, except in Customs and Excise and Immigration Department).
    (b) Nigeria Union of Civil Service Typists, Stenographic and Allied Staff.
(3) Council III
    (a) Civil Service Technical Workers Union of Nigeria
    (b) Medical and Health Workers Union of Nigeria
    (c) National Association of Nigerian Nurses and Midwives
    (d) Printing and publishing Workers Union.
    (e) Customs and Excise and Immigration Staff Union.

It is important to point out that while negotiations take place in the private sector on a regular basis, the same thing cannot be said of the public sector. In spite of the existence of the appropriate machineries, there is not much bargaining in the public sector, including the educational sector. What obtains is the practice by government to unilaterally fix wages and other conditions of work through wage commissions and tribunals as well as the use of tripartite committees whose decisions are still subject to official ratification.

In the education sector, the various unions have often forced the government to negotiate with them. At times, it is not until the unions go on strike that government agrees to negotiate. In the absence of a standing negotiating body what obtains is the appointment of *ad hoc* government negotiating teams, lacking the power to even commit government during negotiations. On occasions, after agreements are reached implementation committees are set up again and in the process fresh challenges are thrown up. What this suggests is a reluctance of government to submit to a basic industrial relations process and it is not unconnected with the failure of government to separate its role as an employer of labour from that of a sovereign authority. This partly explains the failure of the collective bargaining machinery in the public sector with the attendant disruption of services across sectors by workers making legitimate demands. The least government can do is to put in place a standing negotiating structure (instead of the prevailing ad-hoc arrangement) in the education sector, comprising both the government and the union sides. More importantly, this structure should be used regularly while agreements reached should be respected by both sides.

Since wage-related issues are usually involved in virtually all the strike action, including pay relativity among the various categories of workers in the sector, it is appropriate to address this issue. To say that the worker works to earn a decent wage to take care of his/her basic needs should become beyond debate. This was implied in the position of Adam Smith, by no means a radical, that "a man must always live by his work and his wages must at least be sufficient to maintain him" (quoted by Ekundare, 1972: 158). This explains why it is a constant source of disagreement and friction between workers and their employers. It is therefore important that apart from ensuring what people get is commensurate with their efforts, there is also the consideration that the earnings of a worker should guarantee for him/her a decent and humane existence.

It is therefore necessary, at least for the sake of industrial peace, for government to go beyond ad-hocism and unilateralism in wage determination of wages, not only in the education sector, but in the public service as a whole. Apart from procedural issues, wage-fixing should be based on some scientific and verifiable criteria. Among others, the following should determine what workers earn; changes in the cost of living, wage differentials, nature/content of jobs and comparable pay within the economy and the world education system. To address the demand of the non-academic staff for pay parity, the National Salaries, Wages and Incomes Commission should be asked to do a job analysis of component jobs within the sector with a view to determining their relative worth and appropriate compensation. Lastly, there should be wage indexation in order to address unanticipated changes in the prices of goods and services and to forestall avoidable agitations by workers and their unions. The education sector is far too important to be turned into a permanent theatre of conflict. Government should accept that workers, within or outside the trade union, have a right to negotiate terms and conditions with employers. The least that is expected in a democratic polity is for government to respect this right.

Medical Sector

This sector has as its nucleus a handful of teaching and public hospitals in 1960s and 1970s, numbering some 52 in 2010, and joined subsequently by a few medical research and allied institutions.

Till recently, climate and reactions in the medical sector were no different than in other parastatals struggling for improved earnings within the unified salary structure erected by the 1974 Udoji Commission, entry point being a bone of contention between fresh doctors and trained nurses in the 1970s and 1980s in particular. The larger turnover of fresh doctors by increasing number of medical schools and faculties, poor earnings and grossly inadequate facilities saw the massive emigration of doctors in the core structural adjustment years (1987-1994). The professional association, Nigerian Medical Association (NMA), was unable to provide the sort of support needed, and in any case, there was dissension with its ranks regarding tactics and strategies to adopt towards employers and official health sector policies. In the end, the younger doctors formed the National Association of Resident Doctors (NARD) to more effectively promote and protect their interests.

As may be expected, the nurses and other paramedics were the first to form their associations, which were brought under the Medical and Health Workers Union, the National Association of Nigeria Nurses and Midwives, Senior Staff Association of Universities, Teaching Hospitals, Research & Associated Institutions (SS); National Association of

Community Health Practitioners; Nigerian Union of Pharmacists, Medical Technologists & Profession Allied To Medicine (NUPMTPAM) since the 1976-77 restructuring exercise which created separate unions for senior staff and junior staff respectively.

Strikes and other forms of industrial conflict have been caused by the following:

- size of basic salaries;
- arrears or backlog of salaries and allowances due to a) irregularity in payment; and b) delayed implementation of new rates (e.g., in April the NARD called for a nationwide strike to force the Federal Government to implement the Consolidated Medical Salary Structure (CONMESS) and the payment of its arrears from January 2010. The CONMESS was itself a product of long-running negotiations amidst occasional work stoppages over several years;
- relativities;
- out-dated facilities (Besides the implementation of CONMESS, NARD wants the government to improve facilities and adequately staff the hospitals so as to stop oversees medical treatment for affluent citizens. It also seeks the introduction of mandatory post-Part I overseas clinical attachment for resident doctors, as well as budgetary provision for training of members to improve the quality of specialist doctors; and
- the harassment of union officials by law enforcement agents.

Categories of Struggle-tactics

a) Petitions and graffiti

The culture of petition-writing in the public services is deeply ingrained, and graffiti defacing toilet facilities, walls, and other surfaces widely practised. Signed and unsigned letters of protests, authored by individuals and groups transmit a good deal of accurate and false information on all manner of issues to various authorities, local and international mass media and organisations. It is thought that the EFCC, SSS and other security agencies depend substantially on these to initiate investigations.

b) Sympathetic or Sympathy strikes and protests

Most strikes in the federal public service come under this category for a combination of reasons:

a. affected group or groups of workers, except for those strategically located in the operations of the ministry or department or agency, may not be able to muster sufficient disruptive potential to get "management" to look into grievances or demand, so they try to involve other groups of employees;

b. Where Branch Unions exist, to make the industrial action more effective and redress the imbalance in power between it and management, the National Secretariat is necessarily brought into the conflict. And when this occurs, to maximise the impact of the industrial action, the National Secretariat draws in all other branches, thereby inflicting "collateral damage" on other agencies whose workers had no grievances or demands in the first place and thus widening the conflict zone. Put differently, in unionised establishments, sympathy industrial actions tend to predominate because of the structure of the union, which in turn dictates the pattern of mobilisation.

c) Warning strike/Lightning strike

This category comes a close second, especially in the last twenty years. As their names indicate, they are often utilised as bargaining chips, added pressure on management side or government to show seriousness of intention to 'fight' over an issue which, available evidence confirm, that has been left unattended despite series of talks, petitions, etc. They are by nature of brief duration, intense and total.

d) Working-to-rule, go-slow, sit-down strike, stay-home

Again, this category of industrial action ranges from actual stoppage of work (stay away), or slowing down work enough to reduce productivity to a level management should find unacceptable. The stay-away was adopted more frequently during military regimes when overt protests attracted brutal and often violent reaction from law enforcement agencies.

d) General strike

These are few and far between, especially those involving all sectors of the economy for, in a much narrow sense, work stoppage affecting all establishments in an industry may also be dubbed a mini-general strike. Quite often such engulfs the whole economy as unions mobilise across sectors - sympathy actions. More widespread stoppages occurred over the SAP years (1987-1993) and President Obasanjo's unilateral increases in the pump prices of refined petroleum products deregulation and privatisation policies between 2000 and 2005. Same were re-enacted on the two occasions when President Goodluck Jonathan's government increased fuel prices, the last on 2015.

Causes of Industrial Actions

i) Wage-fixing mechanism

The greatest protest-inducing factor in the federal public service is the mechanism for fixing wages. When wages and salaries commissions were the favourite mode for wage-fixing, there were some inputs from all stakeholders (in the form of memoranda, so-called position papers, and physical appearances before them), aside from tripartite composition of most of them. In-between establishment of these wages commissions were period characterised by mounting agitation for review of wages and salaries. And, as noted above, their awards and White Paper on them served to trigger further rounds of strikes and protests.

The post-Wages Commissions era (since mid-1980s) that has seen neo-liberal policies ushered in by variants of SAPs, wage-fixing has remained substantially done administratively, with workers' and unions' resistance introducing a small measure of "negotiations" – that is, reacting to federal government-determined quantum of wages and range of fringe benefits. As noted earlier, the National Negotiating Councils have hardly originated any wage structure; functioned rather like clearing houses for government's guidelines and policies.

By 1998 the Committee on Harmonization of Public Service

Remuneration reorganized the thirty-five different salary structures in the public service into five broad salary structures for all ministries, extra-ministerial departments, agencies, military, police and para-military services and parastatals whose personnel costs are fully funded by the federal government. These are:

i.   Harmonised Public Service Salary Structure (HAPSS) – for the civil service and extra-ministerial departments, all non-commercialised agencies/organizations which were operating the Unified Grading and Salary Structure (UGSS) in any part of the civil service, medical/dental/veterinary doctors in the civil service currently on Medical Salary Structure (MSS/MSSS), all judicial posts which were formerly on GL12 – 17 before the introduction of Judicial Salary Structure, all non-judicial posts of the judiciary, and all staff of primary schools and federal secondary schools;

ii. Harmonised Tertiary Institutions Salary Structure (HATISS) – for all staff of the federal universities, polytechnics, colleges of education, all research institutes and all institutes and agencies formerly operating the Elongated University Salary Structure (EUSS), and all medical doctors in teaching and specialist hospitals, federal medical centres and health agencies;

iii. Harmonised Police and Para-Military Salary Structure (HAPPSS) – for the Nigeria Police, Customs, Immigration and Prison Services, the National Drug Law Enforcement Agency; and the Security Services. But, within a short period the medical personnel in all these agencies opted out for the HATISS;

iv. Harmonised Armed Forces Salary Structure (HAFSS), for the Army, Navy and Air Force personnel; and

v.   Harmonised Top Public Office Holders Salary (TOPSAL) – for the Executive, the Legislative and top judicial personnel.

What still remains unclear is the role of the National Salaries, Incomes & Wages Commission (NSIWC) in wage-fixing for the federal public service, that of the Revenue Mobilisation, Allocation and Fiscal Commission (RMAFC) which, as clearly stated among four other functions, "is to determine the remuneration appropriate to political officer holders." The salaries of officer holders in relation to the rest of the public service suggest the RMAFC has adopted unusual criteria in fixing or recommending such salary structure to approving authorities, one of the assumptions presumably being political officer holders are not in the federal public service! Aside from the outlandish salaries of political officer holders recommended by this agency, there is little reason, giving its essential activity as reflected in its name, for the RMAFC to engage in wage-fixing of any sort and that function should be removed.

According to its website, National Salaries, Incomes and Wages Commission:

1) advises the Federal Government on national incomes policy;

2) recommends the proportions of income growth which shall be utilised for general wage increase;

3) informs the Federal Government of current and incipient trends in wages and proposes guidelines within which increase in wages shall be confined;

4) keeps the Federal Government informed on a continuous basis of movement of all forms of income and propose guidelines relating to profits, dividends and all incomes other than wages;

5) encourages research on wage structure (including industrial, occupational and regional and any other similar factor), income distribution and household consumption patterns;

6) keeps prices under continuous surveillance, interprets price movements and relates them to other developments in the national economy;

7) proposes measures for the regulation of prices and wages in the various sectors of the economy and for the control of hoarding;

8) encourages and promotes schemes for raising productivity in all sectors of the economy;

9) establishes and runs a data bank or other information centre relating to data on wages and prices or any other variable and for that purpose to collaborate with data

collection agencies to design and develop an adequate information system;

10) informs and educates the public on prices, wages and productivity, their relationships with one another and their inter-play in determining standards of living and real economic growth;

11) examines and advises on any matter referred to it by the Federal and State Governments concerning any of the functions conferred on it by or pursuant to the Act;

12) examines, streamlines and recommends salary scales applicable to each post in the public service;

13) examines areas in which rationalisation and harmonisation of wages, salaries and other conditions of employment are desirable and feasible as between the public and private sectors of the economy and recommends guidelines which will ensure sustained harmony in work compensation policies in both the public and private sectors;

14) examines the salary structures in the public and private sectors and recommends a general wage framework with reasonable features of relativity and maximum levels which are in consonance with the national economy;

15) examines and recommends effective machinery for assembling data on a continuing basis taking into account changes in the cost of living, productivity levels, levels of pay in the private sector and other relevant economic data on which public sector salary and other benefits can be reviewed annually;

16) examines the current rate of retirement benefits and recommends appropriate mechanism for periodic review of retirement benefits;

17) inquires into and makes recommendations on any other matter which, in the opinion of the Commission, appear to be relevant to the foregoing and therefore ought, in the public interest, to be inquired into; and

18) undertakes any other activity which is likely to assist in the performance of the functions conferred on it by or pursuant to this Act.

From this impressive list of wage-related activities, especially 3), 12), 13) and 14), the Commission still does not appear to be in a position to *fix wages* but only tinkers with what is handed to it by higher authorities. Which then raises the critical distinction between *negotiating bodies* and *approving authorities*; it is beginning to look like *approving authorities* have become last line "negotiators", their preferences provoking more industrial action until another set of compromises is reached – by trial of strength and politically!

Lack of mandate/ ad hoc official negotiating teams

This brings us to two related variables: i) the apparent lack of mandate; and ii) ad hoc official negotiating teams. It is probably sophistry to say there is a mandate for an inter-ministerial negotiating team, and yet negotiated agreements are subjected to further review by other unseen individuals or committees, especially the Presidency and Mr President himself. No faster way to instigate industrial action than this! On the other hand, the composition of some ad hoc official negotiating teams seems more of political and social posturing, the technocrats and few experts greatly overshadowed by political nominees. Top member of the official negotiating team saying to the Press that "I cannot present this to Mr President" can hardly negotiate in good faith and professionally. What has imagined expectations of Mr President got to do with troubling relativities in pay and inadequate salaries and wages and comparative data that negotiators are addressing?

Trigger mechanism

All these then tie-in to what I call lack of "trigger mechanism". If wages are not indexed, and annual salary increments (ranging ₦100 to ₦500, depending on level and step) are not large enough to offset rate of inflation, what then triggers a review of wages and salaries? Of what use are those surveys conducted and advice offered by the NSIWC if salaries and wages stay the same for a decade and more, except for these annual increments and a handful of persons that may be promoted? This is one reason why the *quantum* of wages/salary and range of fringe benefits, even with so-called monetisation, have always instigated industrial action.

Manner of implementing awards and new salary scales

A related conflict-inducing practice is the apparent lackadaisical approach to implementing awards and new wage/salary scales when finally approved. In many cases, however, the budgetary process may serve to create that impression, when new awards or new salary scales have not been budgeted for, or when statutory allocations are not released in a timely fashion to MDAs. Arrears accumulate and warning and lightning strikes take place, followed subsequently by more widespread work stoppages.

And what hastens this deterioration in labour relations is the absence of the traditional role of "management" in most MDAs. The "management" of any ministry does not see its future tied to how well it "manages" the ministry, or that the welfare and meeting the career expectations of its staff are its responsibility. In any case, most of the staff are employed by another body (Public/Civil Service Commission, Police Service Commission, etc.) and may be redeployed to another MDA without reference to "management". The motivational apparatus is then reduced to wage/salary increases, devoid of other morale, loyalty and productivity boosting policies as prevails on the private sector. This leaves the field wide open to alternative loyalty structures of the trade unions, where they exist.

Union tactics and strategies

In terms of vying for and commanding the respect and loyalty of public servants organised by trade unions, "managements" of most MDAs (again, except for the few that enjoy a degree of institutional autonomy - e.g. educational and oil and gas sectors) are not in the race at all. Given all of the above, some trade union officials have come to believe that the federal government only does what is expected of it when faced by industrial action. Indeed, like ASUU, trade unions look beyond respective "managements" for solutions and negotiations.

Management style

Many parastatals are managed autocratically, several director generals, executive secretaries and managing directors behaving like tin-gods, especially where trade unions do not exist (e.g. the Mint in the 1970s and 1980s). Quite a few industrial actions have been occasioned by poor and authoritarian management styles.

Groups most involved

As may be expected, public servants at the lower rungs of the hierarchy as a group have been the most involved in industrial actions because of economic hardship and less purchasing power. Hence minimum wage, re-grading, and niggardly implementation of new awards lead to disputes and industrial actions so readily.

While, in terms of occupational categories, the artisanal groups across parastatals and ministries, the 'technical', are most active in unionism and protests. This appears to explain why essential services, which tend to have largest contingent of them, are so strike-prone in spite of provisions of the law. Of the senior public servants, again the professionals (doctors, engineers, lawyers, accountants, etc., feel more aggrieved, their counterparts in the private sector obviously the better remunerated also.

A third group would be union members. Grievances are better articulated in organised establishments, and conflict-regulation also routinised or institutionalised as trade union officials carry out their representational functions before management. It is thus a moot point whether the presence of trade unions increases the propensity to industrial action of members. Those who anti-unionism and authoritarian in outlook believe so, much against the insight that trade union officials are "managers of discontent", sandwich as they are between rising expectations of members and those of management. In the Nigerian case, this should require further investigation, but most employers in the oil and gas industry seem to appreciate the restraining role of the unions in the occurrence of and resolution of industrial disputes.

General Recommendations

A. The existing labour law contain statutory provisions that are in violation of the fundamental principles of collective bargaining. Amending relevant sections of the labour law, especially the Trade Disputes Act and Trade Union Act;

1. The "no strike" clause in the Trade Disputes (Essential Services) Act 1976 which outlaws strike actions should be reviewed. The workers covered by the no-strike law are too many - e.g. teachers in *tertiary education* and employees of telecommunications companies in the private sector are included in this category - indicating, as mentioned regarding the Obasanjo (1977) and Abacha regimes, the self-serving political usage of this law rather than the furtherance of less adversarial relations at work in the numerous parastatals defined as "essential services" and without which many ministries cannot meet their mandates;

2. Decree No 4 created a lack of clarity of union' jurisdiction caused by the reduction of 41 trade unions to 29;

3. Trade Union Act proclaiming the NLC and TUC as the only recognised federation of workers violates the principle of freedom of association;

4. Introduce and legally define "unfair labour practices" in the labour law;

5. Introduction of provisions for recognising collective agreements in the court of law;

6. Reducing the overwhelming powers of the Registrar of Trade Unions to unilaterally determine the fate of trade unions;

7. Reviewing the extensive procedures/conditions in the law for the registration of trade unions whose net effect is discouraging, if not rendering impossible, voluntary mergers and formation of federations.

B. Inappropriate, inadequate or dysfunctional collective bargaining units/structures.

- The Federal Government constitutes both "employer" and "sovereign" power, acts as arbiter in a case in which it is a party and creates the impression that it can "do and undo" due to ownership of both financial and sovereign powers, thus restricting the development of collective bargaining. There should be a clear separation of political sovereignty from employer role.
  o Political leadership (President, Minister, relevant Committees of the National Assembly, etc.) should refrain from announcing awards, new allowances and new salary scales for real or perceived political gains. Such should be left to the "technical" bodies and agencies (e.g. NSIWC, National Negotiating Councils).
  o Negotiating bodies should be permanent, and membership not to include political office holders nor officials of political parties
  o The Conciliation and Arbitration institutions should be autonomous, possibly in a new Labour Relations Commission. This would require a new Act.
  o Referral of cases for arbitration should be open to all the parties, not subject to Minister of Labour's approval.

C. Bargaining units have largely been forged by political confrontation than by functionality. The National Negotiating Councils should be restructured and empowered to conduct and conclude all matters relating to wages and salaries.

D. The deregulation of wages has since 1991 been implemented in an ad hoc manner leading to avoidable conflict situations, and should thus be formally institutionalised.

   i. National Council of States should deliberate and formally accept the deregulation of wages to reflect varying capacities to pay of federal, state and local governments.
   ii. This should be incorporated in the Fiscal Responsibility Bill or Act
   iii. Basic rates should be negotiated with workers and their trade unions.
   iv. In MDAs not organised by trade unions, emoluments should be determined by the NSIWC, benchmarking earnings in

comparators in other sub-sectors of the federal public service. The NSIWC should recommend wages of political officer holders to the National Assembly for approval, not the Revenue Mobilisation, & Revenue Allocation Commission (RMAFC) as currently practised.

E. Wages and salaries and other money benefits (before and after monetisation) are not protected against political/administrative interference in terms of regularity of payment, inflation, and quantum. The processes and institutions for the determination and payment of emoluments should be streamlined:

   i.   funds for emoluments should be protected constitutionally against viament

   ii.   The Federal Ministry of Finance and other MDAs involved in the audit of revenue release of statutory allocations be made to do so timely at the risk of sanctions against officers whose responsibility is to do so.

   iii.   The Office of the Head of Service and the NSIWC to conduct quarterly survey of manner of release of statutory allocations.

F. The timing of negotiations and concluding of agreements account for an overwhelming number of disputes and conflicts in the federal public service, and so the timing of negotiations and concluding of agreements should be rationalised:

   i. the expiration of collective agreements, where they exist, should coincide with the end of the financial year;

   ii. as far as is practicable, implementation of new awards, salary scales, allowances, etc., should align with the budgetary process for provisions to be made;

   iii. financial obligations falling due between budgets should be provided for in supplementary budgetary allocation, a process the Presidency and the National Assembly should complete speedily.

G. Existing machinery for negotiations are largely underutilised and preference is for ad hoc bodies. The government should be procedurally and legally compelled to ensure the empowerment and full utilisation of existing machinery for negotiations;

a. The National Negotiating Councils I, II and III to have the mandate of full-blown negotiating machinery;

b. Committee of Vice Chancellors to negotiate with ASUU, while individual Governing Councils sort out peculiar issues with local ASUU branches;

c. A committee of Registrars/Bursars, advised by the Federal Ministry of Education, and the National Universities Commission, and the NSIWC to negotiate with all the Unions of non-academic staff in the universities to establish basic rates for all cadres;

d. the various employee unions in the tertiary institutions should with respective Governing Councils/Boards as the employer constitute themselves into bargaining units to negotiate other terms of employment peculiar to each institution;

e. A committee of Rectors/Provosts, advised by the Federal Ministry of Education, the National Board for Technical Education (NBTE), National Universities Commission, and the NSIWC, to negotiate with all the Unions organising academic and non-academic staff in the polytechnics, colleges of education, and other tertiary institutions not in the university system.

H. Negotiations/Mandate

Most official negotiators are selected on an ad hoc basis, with no or non-binding mandates. The selection of official negotiating teams and conduct of negotiations must be professionalized:

i) Political officer holders should not be members of negotiating team.

ii) Official negotiators should not only be drawn from designated MDAs, but also from specific sections that would be involved in implementation.

iii) Each member of the team should have an appropriate skill, not nominated because he or she is in the good books of the permanent secretary or the director general;

iv) Mandates must be given. This should eliminate by the lack of good faith bargaining whereby public sector employers conclude negotiations which they have no intention to honour or sustain, or initiate negotiations in which the government This has resulted in creating the negative impressions/ perception and distrust largely from such unwillingness (not inability) to implement agreements;

v) Probably duration of negotiations should be part of the mandate;

vi) An agreement that is negotiated and signed should not be upturned, as there is enough time during negotiations for consultations on concessions with approving authorities to take place

I.   Implementation style

Implementation of decisions, agreements, and understandings are largely arbitrary, not consistent and generate a lot of conflict and loss of confidence in the system:

i) multiple approving authorities should be reduced in number, and clearly identified

ii) some members of an inter-ministerial or White Paper drafting committee, or relevant approving agencies, should sit in at negotiations and thus not undo all the findings and recommendations of negotiators and experts, a seeming habit that has so destabilised the system to date. Their decisions should be based on benchmarks and other data provided by negotiators, and not personal preferences and/or because such individuals have the ears of those who give final approval.

iii) the Federal Ministry of Finance has to release funds in a timely fashion, and made aware of the deleterious effects of not doing so – and sanctions should be imposed on erring official.

iv) commencement of implementation (new allowances, salary scale, grading, etc.) should be negotiated, tied to the budget, and not form part of political promises of any political office holder (the 'political' credit shall still go to the incumbent when implemented anyway).

J. Trigger Mechanism/Frequency of Review

How and when to initiate a review of wages and salary structure remain arbitrary and are conflict-generating. The review of wages/salary structure in the federal public service should be institutionalised, routinised so as to stabilise the system and generate commitment, and enhance morale:

a)   There should be yearly increments in basic rates of at least 10 per cent to offset inflation and ensure competitiveness, without prejudice to steps in respective scales which themselves are grossly insufficient till a general review is undertaken as currently practised.

b)   The NSIWC to compute and issue circular.

c)   A General Wages/salaries review every 2 or 3 years. The National Negotiating Councils should be empowered and expanded to include NSIWC, independent experts and the Nigerian Industrial & Employment Relations Association.

d)   Presidency, National Assembly to facilitate any new Act

K. Status of Collective Agreements

Voluntarily derived Collective Agreements are not fully respected, thereby generating conflict situations and chronic instability in public sector industrial relations, as well as impacting negatively on legitimacy and goodwill of Government. Collective Agreements should be binding on all parties. The best international practice is for collective agreements to be justiciable, the courts imposing penalties, discipline and responsible behaviour on all parties and thus reducing considerably occasions for widely destabilising conflicts. Amending relevant sections of the Employment Act, review of the powers of both the IAP and NIC should they not be replaced by a Labour Relations Commission. The Presidency, National Assembly and Federal Ministry of Justice to facilitate implementation.

L. Tertiary Education/Research Institutions, etc.

A disproportionate proportion of disputes occur in Educational and related institutions, especially over wages/salaries, arrears and inadequate facilities. A holistic approach to wage bargain and negotiation institutions and processes is overdue. They should be completely overhauled:

1. A committee of Vice Chancellors, advised by the Federal Ministry of Education, the National Universities Commission, and the NSIWC should negotiate with ASUU to establish basic rates for all categories of academic staff in the universities;

2. A committee of Registrars/Bursars, advised by the Federal Ministry of Education, and the National Universities Commission, and the NSIWC to negotiate with all the Unions of non-academic staff in the universities to establish basic rates for all cadres;

3. the various employee unions in the tertiary institutions should with respective Governing Councils/Boards as the employer constitute themselves into bargaining units to negotiate other terms of employment peculiar to each institution;

4. A committee of Rectors/Provosts, advised by the Federal Ministry of Education, the National Board for Technical Education (NBTE), National Universities Commission, and the NSIWC, to negotiate with all the unions organising academic and non-academic staff in the polytechnics, colleges of education, and other tertiary institutions not in the university system;

5. First, funding of facilities must be improved upon, matching international best practice represented by UNESCO recommended budgetary ratio;

6. Second, for current levels of and improved funding to be more effective and eliminate acrimonies and conflicts over relativities and mounting labour costs and other administrative overheads to the detriment of teaching and research facilities in this sector, a deadline of a maximum of three years (various tertiary administrations have been deliberately avoiding this) must be enforced by relevant regulatory authorities (NUC, etc.) for tertiary institutions to comply with a mandatory maximum Academic-Non-Academic Staff ratio. This is the best practice internationally; the smaller the ratio, the more cost-effective funding becomes as a good many services are outsourced, thereby reducing the fully engaged, pensionable "support staff" to a bare minimum;

7. To accelerate the supply of much-need teaching and technical staff, a) the federal government must increase its funding of postgraduate training locally and abroad; b) universities should be made to increase the intake ratio of undergraduate-postgraduate students in favour of the latter within a short period; c) local and foreign companies and agencies offering scholarships be encouraged to concentrate more on postgraduate training; d) state and local governments should also be

encouraged to spend more on postgraduate training (bursaries, scholarships, loans, etc.); and e) the enforcement of bonds of recipients for sponsorship be improved upon and they be employed or placed in tertiary educational and research institutions.

M. Medical and allied sectors

The medical and allied sectors have continually been plagued by issues of inadequate facilities, grading, relativities and arrears of salaries and wages and allowances. Wage determination institutions and processes in the medical and allied sectors are to be revamped:

1. strengthening Council III which has the two unions representing medical and health workers and nurses and midwives respectively
2. Increased funding and equipping of medical institutions
3. Liaising more effectively with the National Association of Resident Doctors
4. Federal Government to implement the Consolidated Medical Salary Structure (CONMESS)

N. Oil and Gas Sector

Employment relations are generally less conflict-driven in the oil and gas sector, conflicts occurring over the years due to opposition to specific official policies:

I. the federal government must carry the unions along in its policy implementation by holding effective consultations on its planned deregulation of downstream petroleum sector and also in the privatization of public enterprises in the oil and gas sector.

II. the communication channel used by government must be effective to forestall misinterpretation and misrepresentation of government's intention by the mass media and the public which could generate uncertainty and crisis, e.g. the tension generated by the rumour of government's proposed relocation of PTI in Warri to Kaduna.

III. All parties should respect collective agreement by implementing it to the letter.

O. Recruitment/Relativities

The widespread abuse of the Federal Character Principle (most especially under military regimes) and the introduction of other socio-political consideration in recruitment, placement, promotion and retrenchment of federal public servants have led to over-manning, low morale, low motivation, increasing incompetence, and declining productivity. Recruitment, placement, promotion and disengagement procedures and processes should be professionalized:

a) All prospective candidates should sit an examination, and subjected also to other forms of evaluation (e.g. interview);

b) Minimum entry qualification should be a good first degree, with the exception of clearly identified technical posts for which minimum entry may be OND. This should reduce conflicts over differentials and career path on this score;

c) Placement and promotion should be based on such objective criteria as skills, appropriate experience, competence, formal qualifications and performance at written examinations. In a politicised public service, down-grading objective criteria (e.g. examinations) in favour of superiors' subjective assessment of subordinates is retrograde and is no way to create efficient and productive federal public servants for the challenges of the twenty-first century;

d) The relevant sections of the Constitution may have to be amended to guarantee that "quota recruitment" ceases to translate into "quota placement", "quota promotion" and "quota disengagement" because competent hands can be found in all corners of the country.

P. Managing Function

Most managements in MDA have not developed competent Industrial Relations and Human Resource Management Skills. The HR/IR management functions in MDAs should be improved upon:

a) a cadre of Industrial Relations/HR officers, like other professionals in the public service (doctors, accountants, lawyers, etc.) should be specially trained and deployed to all MDAs;

b) such officers should be in regular consultation (weekly or bi-monthly or monthly audit meetings) with respective managements of MDAs;

c) the Federal Ministry of Labour in conjunction with NIRA, NECA, Department of Employment Relations & Human Resource Management of the University of Lagos, and ASCON should initiate 'crash' and other training programmes for prospective IR/HR officers.

Q. Pension

The funding and administration of pension have continued to generate anxieties among public servants. Government to fine-tune the funding and administration of pension:

i.   the irregular payment of pension must cease;
ii.   the privatisation of the management of pension funds should be partial (e.g. mandatory investment in Treasury bills) as measure for protecting pensioners against pension funds managers going out of business

R. Respect for the rule of law

Both employers and workers and their trade unions tend, on several occasions, not to respect the rule of law. The rule of law as it applies to parties in the public sector industrial relations system should be upheld and enforced:

1) mediation, conciliation and arbitration processes should be insulated from political pressures of MDAs and the Federal Government as employers by increasing their autonomy;

2) "No work, no pay" provision in the Trade Disputes Act should be more rigorously enforced;

3) Similarly, "No pay, no work" should be enforced as it is also a violation of the contract of employment and the law on contracts, and does not accord with best practice;

4) Arrears of salaries, wages, and allowances should attract legal sanctions, just as directors and managements in private sector corporate bodies can be sanctioned by the law, the same should apply to erring MDAs. It is not enough to seek parity in earnings with private sector, and yet abandon accountability and responsibilities that prevail there and which ensure higher levels of productivity;

5) Wages, salaries and other emoluments should receive legal protection, even if such involves the introduction of a justiciable clause in the Constitution (granted same status as revenue allocation formula, federal character principle, etc.);

6) Some statutory instruments setting up MDAs may be amended accordingly;

7) The arbitrariness of law enforcement agencies (e.g. police, intelligence agencies) in apprehending disputes, aborting brewing disputes, and in their dealings with trade union officials and some workers generally should be stopped. Aside from breaching fundamental human rights in the process, reinforcing through their actions authoritarian, incompetent and sometimes corrupt "managements" of some MDAs merely serve to accentuate difficulties, exacerbate conflicts and perpetuate unstable and magnified adversarial industrial relations in the federal public sector.

S. The Federal Ministry of Labour

The activities of the Ministry are critical to the sustenance of less adversarial public sector industrial relations, a role that has been largely inhibited by lack of human and non-human resources. The federal government to specially fund and equip the Ministry to render more effective services:

i)   Special recruitment of specialists by the Civil Service Commission

ii) Short-term training programmes locally and abroad

iii) Medium-run capacity building for staff in the departments of IR/HR in the universities

iv) Engaging services of experts/consultants

v)   Expanding scope for ADR options

vi) Special funds to facilitate mediatory efforts of labour officers

vii) Crash programme for short-term production/training of Factory Inspectors

viii) Immediate capacity building for the National Productivity Centre – to conduct regular productivity surveys, among its other functions.

Final destination?

Depending on the decade, commentaries on and prognoses about employment relations and political developments in Nigeria and Africa generally might be grouped under two broad categories, Marxism-inclined and the eclectic. The "revolutionary potentials" of workers and their trades unions featured mostly in the period 1950 to 1970s, when dominant conservative groups and forces tried to contain or redirect ideological ferment in Europe and North America themselves, decolonisation itself feared to have enormous potential for revolutionary options. The variants of African Socialisms which dotted the African political landscape, from Ghana, Guinea in West Africa, Angola, Mozambique in Eastern Africa to Tanzania in Southern Africa, were probably richer in practice and ideas on stratified communalism than socialism-communism of the sort Karl Marx and his followers advocate. Rationalisations or denunciations of relative paucity of revolutionary movements have ranged from:

i) dominance of "false consciousness" (which argues of material, ideological and institutional processes in capitalist society misleading the "proletariat" and its logical allies regarding exploitative nature of arrangements);

ii) limited "class consciousness" (as exploited groups or classes view and react to their circumstances as individuals), a failure to see oneself as a part of a class with particular class interests relative to the economic order and social system and thus failing to collectively confront and overthrow exploiters and capitalism;

iii) the structure and workings of the economy, labelled "dependent capitalism", have tended to increase prevalence of the earlier two while intensifying externally-determined exploitation; to

iv) socio-political workings of these societies being determined or held back by "neo-patrimonialism" and "prebendalism", where the former, a concept derived from Max Weber's use of patrimonialism as a form of traditional domination projecting patriarchy and popularised by Shmuel Eisenstadt (1973),[39] as vulgarised stands for a system where prominent or politically well-placed persons personalise state resources and use same to secure the loyalty of clients in the general population, an informal patron-client relationship that can pervade state structures down to individuals in small villages, and latter, again mutated from Weber's use of prebend in his wide-ranging discussion of transition of Europe from patriarch-induced administrative and political domination to more rational, bureaucratic and scientific modes, Richard Joseph has applied to the Nigerian political scene.[40]

Neo-Patrimonialism, Dependent Capitalism and Prebendalism

What *neo-patrimonialism, dependent capitalism* and *prebendalism* have in common, in the context of our Lecture, is their very limited explanatory value, despite their seemingly dutiful use by European and North American social scientists who consider themselves to be specialists on African affairs and "developing areas" generally – not to mention also the amazing appeal of same concepts to the more radical African social scientists. In his tracing of patriarchy and patrimonialism suffusing centuries of European and Asian development (mostly India), Max Weber urged the adoption of procedures embodied in legal-rational bureaucracy[41] as most efficient, most predictable, precise and scientific

---

[39] *Eisenstadt, Shmuel N. (1973). Traditional Patrimonialism and Modern Neopatrimonialism. Beverly Hills: Sage Publications.*

[40] The word "Prebend" came into use in the 15th century when the Catholic Church provided both religious and political headship (the pope) for feudal European principalities, kingdoms, and empires, and being a decentralised arrangement dogged by rivalries and conflicting jurisdictions, a prebend was a position or land or stipend offered to lesser church or other officials to sustain their loyalty. Such a system of building clientelism was described as "prebendary". The Catholic Encyclopedia defines a prebend as the "right of member of chapter to his share in the revenues of a cathedral." Richard A. Joseph, director of The Program of African Studies at Northwestern University at the time, is usually credited with first using the term "prebendalism" to describe patron-client or "neopatrimonialism" in Nigeria. "According to his take on the theory of prebendalism, state offices are regarded as prebends that can be appropriated by officeholders, who use them to generate material benefits for themselves and their constituents and kin groups..." See Joseph, Richard, *Democracy and Prebendal Politics in Nigeria: The Rise and Fall of the Second Republic*, Cambridge University Press, 1987.

[41] The characteristics of Ideal Type Bureaucracy as advocated by Max Weber are i) a) recruitment by ability and technical/formal education qualifications; b) job is a career, full-time; c) bureaucrats are arranged in a hierarchy, according to status; d) the powers and jurisdiction of any position or

tool for domination, vastly superior to earlier forms of traditional and charismatic modes of domination. First, Max Weber was building a model in the ideal-typical sense, isolating those characteristics he considered could reduce, if not eliminate, arbitrariness and personal, family, and subjective influences on how society is administered. Hence Weber wrote about "an ideal type bureaucracy", a model that studies of modern European countries have shown practices not to faithfully approximate.[42]

Second, perhaps more crucially, he was more concerned with the *administrative instrument* deployed by those who politically dominate society, which he sought for them to develop and use in more efficient/scientific fashion, irrespective of their political goals. Weber was convinced *rationality* in human affairs would increase as traditional bureaucratic patrimonial forms of government eventually give way to modern capitalist bureaucratic rationalism as the main principle of both government and governance. *Neo-patrimonialism* as a description of what might be taking place in Nigeria, African countries, etc., stays essentially a modelling process, a condescending and largely inaccurate labelling exercise bereft of any serious explanatory utility – and it is not because I say so. If Nigerian, African societies, for example, are so steeped in neo-patrimonialism and with all the gender, class and generational inequalities such entails (and believe me there are quite a few of these in some social-cultural practices), why would Europeans and North Americans be battling with gender-based pay inequalities in their legal-

---

office are clearly delineated, ensuring specialisation and sphere of competence; e) remuneration is fixed, according to status and position in the hierarchy; f) separation of personal from official means/tools of work; g) emphasis on written communication; h) impersonal relations among bureaucrats, and between them and the public; and i) promotion is based on merit and judgement of superiors. Weber, M., *The Theory of Social and Economic Organisation*, Free Press, 1964 (first published in 1925).

[42] Burrell, G & Morgan, G., *Sociological Paradigms and Organisational Analysis*, Heinemann, London, 1979; Child, J. (ed.), *Man and Organisation*, Allen & Unwin, London, 1973; Clegg, S. & Dunkerley, D., *Organisation, Class and Control*, RKP, London, 1980; Crozier, M., *The Bureaucratic Phenomenon*, Tavistock, London, 1964; Etzioni, E., *Complex Organisations: A Sociological Reader*, Holt & Rinehart, London, 1966; Fox, A., *A Sociology of Industry*, Collier-Macmillan, London, 1971; *Man Mismanagement*, Hutchinson, London, 1974 (2nd edn, 1985); Gouldner, A.W., *The Coming Crisis of Western Sociology* Heinemann, London, 1971; Mouzelis, N.P., *Organisation and Bureaucracy*, RKP, London, 1967

rationally dominated organisational structures but Nigerians and other African countries routinely pay male and female employees same wages/salaries – and this despite the domination of their economies by European and North American companies? And whatever happened to the replicating impacts of institutional transfers? As for nepotism and succession to office, the few examples in Africa - Eyadema in Togo, Kabila in Congo, Kenyatta in Kenya and Gaddafi in Libya - are no different from the Kennedy, Bush, Clinton and Trump families in the United States of America and Trudeau in Canada.

In some ways, *Dependent Capitalism*, conveys a fairly useful impression but tends to the superficial. First, I think the foisting of a binary distinction of "core-periphery" does two things: i) obfuscates the gradations and directions of dependency; the dominant countries or empires in any historical period *depend* on the rest to maintain such position, just as, using current circumstances, the United States, Canadian, British, German, French, Chinese, Indian and Japanese economies depend on each other to varying degrees and there is no one "core". India and China were not labelled "core" three decades ago, so dominant powers do rise and fall in spite of core status; ii) periphery is misused, since any of all the other Asian, South American, African, Middle-Eastern and European economies may in fact be "core", a function of the resources therein critical for the more dominant economies, a factor that plays out in their politics (an aspect of neo-colonialism alluded to earlier) and configures international diplomatic and military strategies, rather than imagined neo-patrimonialism. Second, it attaches too much importance to capitalism as the understated or glossed over element in dependency is *military might*, of which Israel, an instance, is "core" in the Middle East but not for its economic resources, just as Saudi Arabia is "core" for its oil wealth. This logic likely underlies the notion of "world system" as adumbrated upon by Wallerstein and others, rendering concepts as "peripheral capitalism" less than illuminating.[43] From historical evidence since antiquity,

---

[43] Wallerstein, I., *World System Analysis: an Introduction*, Duke University Press, Durham and London, 2004; *The Modern World-System I*; University of California Press, Berkeley and Los Angeles 2011; *Modern World-System II*, University of California Press, 2011; *The Modern World*

dependency has been due to *political* and *military dominance rather than to forms of economic system*, the extent of dominance moderated by state of communications, of transportation and military organisation, and hence centuries of decentralised vassalage and prebends. Same for "under-development", capitalist or otherwise, dominant powers routinely "under-developing" wherever they could to maintain their dominance, the epoch dictating the mode, mechanisms and intensity of such plundering. The dynamics of dominance of the United States of America since the mid-1940s of other Western countries has been little different from that of erstwhile Soviet Union over former Eastern Europe. So is the famously celebrated colonisers' "indirect rule" of reliance on pre-existing administrative and social structures in Africa of the 1900s being one of such misconceptions and modelling outcomes; the coloniser on the most part had no choice because of *distance*, and such has been the case from ancient times, thus Colonel Lugard and his ilks in Nigeria and Africa invented no such thing.

Prebendalism appears to be least illuminating or useful of the three concepts. First, there is no historical survey or analysis of prebends and their use in the massive empires and kingdoms that dotted African landscape before and from the fifteenth century when prebends featured prominently in Mediaeval Europe, a period during which the Oba of Benin exchanged ambassadors with the King of Portugal.

Second, habits do not occur overnight and as has been pretty well documented, common knowledge and sketched out at the beginning of this Lecture, colonialism was by brute force, debasing and corrupting of all pre-colonial institutions and colonisers could not have had the privilege of using prebends since they thrived on arbitrariness, corruption, whims and caprices and that was why barely a decade into the 'amalgamation' of various colonially instituted administrative units in 1914, massive protests right into late 1930s accompanied official attempts at introducing a regime of direct and indirect taxes.[44]

Third, that Nigerian elites occupying public offices personalise state resources and for the use of their "kith and kin" reveals warped rendition

---

System III, Berkeley and Los Angeles, 2011; *The Modern World System IV*, University of California Press, Berkeley and Los Angeles, 2011.

[44] The most violent being the riots in Burutu in 1927 and the Aba Tax Riots in 1928-1929

of the dynamics, as most of such kith and kin are Arab, European and American corporate bodies, business persons and their bankers. Fourth, in a prebendary arrangement of the sort in referent mediaeval Europe, there is always a power-wielding and legitimizing *giver*, in contrast to random *self-constituting* elites as has been the case in Nigeria and inured to gliding from party to party and many of whom lack support of their immediate constituents and kith and kin. Fifth, crucial trade-offs between and among powerful factions of Nigerian elites have proved impressively more successful at managing ethnic and cultural diversities as compared with Europeans and North Americans at any age, the latter, going by antecedents and existing practices, seeming incapable of rising above institutionalised racism in spite of legal-rational bureaucratic ethos.[45] Thus, internally in those countries, xenophobia, ethnic, religious and other social divisions are manifesting at a frightening degree. And, to come closer home to our primary area of focus in this Lecture, whereas Nigerian trades unions have managed multi-ethnicity and multi-culturalism fairly well, some American trade unions are still organised along racial and sub-ethnic lines.

The geo-political space labelled Nigeria is a complex mosaic of cultural practices and political values, including ethnic groups in the south and middle-belt hitherto with no experience of centralised political systems, leaving aside what might have been borrowed or being emulated by state actors, like the institution of political parties which existed from 1860s (Lagos Colony) when many European countries *had none.* Prebendalism does not and cannot offer us an explanation of why the Yoruba family with Christian and Moslem members live peaceably but Hausa and Fulani are daggers-drawn over same although they are kith and kin and with spasmodic "Sharia riots" involving massive loss of lives. It sheds precious little light on why such intense self-focus by self-administered millions of villages, various communities and townsfolk

---

[45] For example, the two Dutch and French-speaking tribes in Belgium are yet to settle; in Spain the Catalans are being smothered; Turks and Greeks in Cyprus; and English are still managing to hold out against the Welsh, Scots and Irish in Britain and Northern Island; the wars that followed the disintegration of Yugoslavia, the most vicious being that of Serbia and the rest in Kosovo environs; Czechoslovakia into Czech and Slovenia; Switzerland divided itself along dominant languages,; the Bavarians and the rest in Germany and so on. And there are hardly important cases of religious, ethnic and political conflicts in Africa not fuelled by external interests.

even within the same clan, nor on the relative indifference to and view of the state as no man's land. Or, why some contestants for local government, or state-wide, national or central positions who fail woefully to muster enough votes from among kith and kin and sub-ethnic group, scale through on the votes garnered among ostensibly bitter rival ethnic groups who are in the same constituency and elsewhere.[46] Nigeria would have since disintegrated where it a European country.

In all this, though, let us clear up one small point: this is no denial or defence of corruption among the political classes in Nigeria or Africa or of attempts to secure votes or political advantage by appeals to "kith and kin" and fellow-tribes people have not occurred in some instances. It is merely to show that prebendalism, as used by its proponents, merely begs the question of national political developments, if not diversionary in intent; at best, it is a simple misapplication of an idea or concept, while at worst, it is modelling of a very tendentious species.

So, in which directions would the Nigerian state, private employers and workers and their organisations be heading?

1. Trades Unions, Trades Unionism and Social consciousness

What we should glean from the immediate above is the immense difficulty of deciphering essential nature of self-identity and social consciousness, both which affect strategies and tactics, bearing in mind especially what managements and trades unions do and how they do what they do in Nigeria and in light of Marx's oft-quoted quip of mode of existence determining one's social consciousness. A run-down of two sectors, education and oil and gas, is presented to provide a backdrop against which a more rewarding appreciation of notions of "proletarian consciousness" and "revolutionary consciousness" may be made.

Education Sector
The education sector tends to bring out the intricacies of inter-elite and intra-elite relations than most, part-fashioning the canvas on which

---

[46] For instance, Presidential candidate General Obasanjo did not win any of the south-west States in 1999, though, going by prebandalism wisdom, the mere fact that he was Yoruba should have guaranteed a victory in all the Southwest or Yoruba-speaking States, his natural ethnic-regional base. Instead, he was voted into power by other Nigerians from the East and North.

trades unions draw their own designs. It comprises primary schools, secondary schools, colleges of education, polytechnics and universities, with managements drawn from local governments, state governments, federal government and private investors. The Nigerian Union of Teachers has primary and secondary institutions is its constituency, while several trades unions draw membership from tertiary education institutions as outlined earlier. For lack of space, we use the tertiary education subsector for illustration purposes.

The physical location of tertiary education institutions, especially universities, has become subject to more blatant parochial and political considerations and, when successfully done, it becomes one of the touted achievements by a faction of the traditional and political elites in their rivalry. Subsequent concessions gained by them would cover the whole gamut of running the affected institution: recruitment, selection and placement of principal officers, contracts, admissions, examinations, promotions, to disciplinary issues of staff and students, the selection/appointment of the vice chancellor, registrar, deans and heads of departments, the push being for "daughters" and "sons" of the soil/locality or ethnic group. All of these obviously serve to condition the environment, comportment, conduct of, and tactics adopted by, personnel within these institutions in achieving their private and parochial objectives.

Another aspect of the competition over physical location of universities (senatorial district, geo-political zone, state, local government, etc.) – read tertiary institutions - is the hurried establishment of so many, with or without the approval of the National Universities Commission and other education regulatory agencies, fed by grossly inadequate funding, little physical and other infrastructure, poor staffing, poorly-built, poorly-equipped laboratories and lecture rooms, inevitably throw personnel therein into situations of so many aggravating factors, of fluid and barely functioning statutory and standing committees through paucity of numbers, lack of experienced hands and machinations of rival caucuses or groups, many practices hardly reflecting regular university culture and system, and local and political circumstances (e.g. amazingly late and inadequate budgets of federal and state governments) and conduct of traditional and political elite have amplified divisive impacts.

Every now and then and aside from establishment and location of tertiary institutions in particular, traditional and political elites gerrymander the education sector in more destructive fashion, from protesting against West African Examinations Council (WAEC) results, Joint Admissions and Matriculation Board (JAMB) scores, cut-off points, admission quotas, number of professors from their areas of origin, to the fewness of vice chancellors from same. In accommodating some of these demands and in the case of vice chancellors, the phrase "senior academic" has been deliberately and liberally interpreted in a few instances to mean "senior lecturers and above" for senior lecturers to become vice chancellors in a few universities. In such universities, the demand for "democratisation" of the university system translates into senior lecturers, and, in a few cases, lecturer grade one being "elected" heads of department and deans, a sad caricature of the system.

More crucially, Nigeria appears to be the only country were trades unions organising non-academic staff insist on the elimination of the appellation "academic staff" for "teaching staff" in their bid to narrow, if not eliminate, basis of differentials between them and lecturers; several non-academic staff also insisting on their job-functions having "academic" component, in an oblique attack on their status as "support staff" who, in the universities easily outnumber academic staff by a ratio of 10:1, the National Universities Commission recommending a 7:1 ratio. Either option still renders the cost of non-academic personnel too expensive and superfluous while also changing the basic administrative structure with the creation of directorate positions superior to a flush of deputy registrars ensconced in practically all units.

More recently, the Federal Character Commission has been pushing for the right to sit on recruitment interview panels in federally funded tertiary institutions "to ensure fair distribution of positions among states" and, for added measure, it has been alleged, trying to ignore the provisions of statutes establishing these educational institutions as self-regulating corporate bodies and wanting private contracts between them and professors set aside to enable it supervise the random posting of professors to any institution!

2. Oil and Gas sector

Here we present results of our surveys in the oil and gas industry for the period 2010 to 2014. Given the somewhat different circumstances in exploration and production, service and marketing/distribution sections of the industry, the findings are not typical of any one company. But the results provide useful information to managements and trade unions alike, shedding some light on why labour relations in the industry are the way they are.

The oil and gas industry itself has different activities, and most of them are *subcontracted* by the oil/gas producing and refined petroleum products-marketing companies. Some of such activities include supplying rigs, barges, vehicles, catering, facility maintenance, generators, spares or parts, construction, transportation, medical, accounting/legal and other consultancy services.

With outsourcing and subcontracting as the dominant means of providing labour, goods and other services, the average employee in the oil and gas industry tends to be preoccupied with job insecurity and career path. The work schedule of most employees in the field or offshore is another challenge, broken into alternating spells of work and off-periods. These and welfare issues and role of expatriates (especially all manner of allowances) tend therefore to feature prominently in negotiations, and substantially determine the morale and productivity of employees as well as attitudes and approaches of branches of NUPENG and PENGASSAN to respective managements.

Host Communities

Host community is the people occupying the area where the business is physically located and has its administrative headquarters, or a unit of the business secures raw material for processing elsewhere. This is a *geographical definition* of "host community", and it may prove insufficient, if not misleading, in our efforts to understand communities' reactions to business and workers' organisations. A *socio-political definition* of "host communities" should include all those who come from the designated area but live and earn a living outside it. In an overwhelming number of cases, those "sons and daughters" who live elsewhere but are well placed in society or politically well-connected, do tend to influence events on the ground by participating in the formulation of "community demands" or what constitutes "development" for their respective communities.

Community may be formed by groups of families, often historically in extended family units to become a lineage and then a clan. A clan may comprise offspring or descendants of persons from the same great, great, great grand-parents and beyond, settled in same area but in different villages and towns. Several clans with common ancestors, language, culture, etc., may become an ethnic group and, in the Nigerian context, administratively or politically grouped in a local government or several local governments. *This means host communities are not homogenous.* Each family, lineage, clan, village, and groups within the same ethnic group have had a long history of social rivalry and conflict, some very bitter and violent and involving neighbours, even cousins, siblings, in-laws, and allies on opposing sides. The creation of State and local government may also fuel rivalry and rekindle old animosities between ethnic groups and clans. It is thus not unusual for some people to devise strategies for the well being and reconstruction of their households over and beyond those for the community. In the post-conflict period relations between people in the area would be shot through with feuds and division relating to the conflict.

To summarise, communities may be formed by: i) refugees; ii) new settlements of migrant workers that grow up around sites, projects, etc.; iii) village or group of villages; iv) clan; v) ethnic group; vi) ethnic groups; vii) local government; viii) a State; ix) groups of states (e.g. South-South); x) a country; and xi) a group of countries. Communities are infused with systems of power, hierarchy, authority and values which define the lives of their members. The social relations between members of the same locality can be overtly hostile. For example, two or more villages may have closer affinity due to long-standing common festivals or rituals of some sort and thus have indifferent to hostile disposition towards those from certain villages, even avoiding marrying from them; some people have returned to their home-villages after the years of displacement into camps or other areas and find themselves living back next to neighbours or even relations who had inflicted violence upon them during the very personal and local violence of the recent past. Such histories, though not overtly mentioned, are remembered and work against collective reconstruction and community development projects.

Community Relations

As part of corporate social responsibility (CSR) and in adapting to local situations most companies in the oil and gas sector have become involved in providing certain services and goods to various communities. From the above, it would appear that a major challenge for the management of community-relations is that the idea of 'community' as advocated in policy by many managements and political authorities is often a simple and romantic notion which is difficult to find, work with and translate into practice.

Community relations have involved the construction of roads, public buildings, markets, jetties, mini-hospitals; funding of self-employment projects, education (structures and scholarships), arts and culture, housing, sport development, environment conservation, policy /research grants to some NGOs and research institutions; award of contracts to some "sons" and "daughters" of host communities, use of local third party providers and subventions to some traditional authorities and youth organisations. Evidently, these corporate social investments have achieved various degree of success in influencing developments on the ground, especially in the Niger Delta.

There are also those businesses, particularly those in relatively isolated and/or rural areas that have relied heavily on local political authorities and influential personalities for conflict regulation purposes. There have been cases where disputes and strikes have been settled at the court of, or by emissaries of, some local chief, *bale, oba* or emir or king: the community must not lose this industry or company has always been the traditional line of argument of such third parties promoting voluntary settlements of disputes between management and employees.

A crucial aspect of community relations projects is their broader impact on respective communities. Even in populations without bitter past history, many companies, government officials and non-governmental organisations find that when they work in a community they are *drawn to one or other segment of the population.* Others in the population may not only just feel disenfranchised from systems of authority and influence, the sponsors of community projects may actually be re-arranging statuses and relative distribution of power and wealth among and between the various components of the community and sections/wards of villages/towns: traditionally more powerful lineages and clans may decline in the new politics of community development, hence "restiveness", and charges of "discrimination", etc., directed at some companies.

What all this amounts to is that the *physical location* of community relations projects and the choice of local contractors to deal with often lead to resurgence of deep and bitter divisions, rivalry and jealousy which still exist between and among many villages and clans and inhabitants. There are sometimes armed, violent conflicts between members of the community, each side accusing the other of trying to gain stronger political influence and having final say over location of projects in particular. In the implementation of some projects, therefore, all participants are unlikely to be equal partners, and some may be actively discriminated against, and may unwittingly lead to the institutionalisation of oppression of various persons, segment of a village or clan. When combined with local political rivalries for traditional titles and elective offices at local, state and federal levels, sporadic outbreaks of tension and violence should not be surprising.

However, as in most things, "community relations" have become a huge phenomenon on their own, a lucrative business for those not too professional but saddled with the responsibility. Quite often, a sub-department handles these matters and is distanced from the HR Department itself, perching between Corporate Affairs and Public Relations where both are separated, or reporting to the office of the chief executive officer. Whatever the internal organisational politics over the organogram, and thus allocation of functions and responsibilities, the management of community relations has multifarious implications for the HR function in businesses or industries where host communities' reactions constitute a significant aspect of the business environment.

Challenges facing union leadership
Trades unions leadership face challenges from several sources and are:

i) Human resource within the trade union, that is, the rank and file.

ii) Those caused by the environment or context within which trade union leadership finds itself. Prominent among these would be the i) nature of the industry, ii) the companies, and iii) nature of the jobs performed by employees and members.

iii) Those created by regulatory authorities and government's socio-economic, industrial and industrial relations policies;

iv) Those from respective oil-bearing communities.

These four categories translate into the following challenges and outcomes:

a) the work force is much younger and better educated;

b) most trade union members are also young;

c) most trade union officers, elected and appointed, are also young;

d) most trade union officers, elected and appointed, are relatively new in their positions and thus have not gained much experience in managing affairs of the union;

e) the administrative and other demands of PENGASSAN are increasing;

f) state of relations between NUPENG and PENGASSAN;

g) members of management are better educated than before;

h) globalisation and the exploitation of 'global resources' have increased the number of transnational companies in the Nigerian economy, companies with vast global connections and using most up-to-date communications technology; and

i) reactions to the current experiment in political party system of political mobilisation and governance.

j) the degree of level of formal education of many union officials;

k) degree of administrative and public relations skills;

l) degree of members' and union officials' familiarity with the history of labour struggles, especially in Nigeria;

m) extent of sound knowledge of the oil and gas industry;

n) extent of negotiating skills;

o) union leadership's capacity for critical analysis and sound judgement;

p) degree of courage, integrity and transparency shown by union leadership; and

q) Degree of democratisation.

Environment or Context

The environment or context within which trades unions leadership finds itself poses several challenges, that include *nature of the industry* with the following characteristics:

i) it is a strategic industry, and has both domestic and international implications;

ii) it is a politically and environmentally sensitive industry and thus attracts both domestic and international attention;

iii) it involves activities directed at locating and exploiting oil and gas deposits, notably seismic surveys, transportation and supply of required equipment, drilling (on shore and off-shore), refining and distribution of refined petroleum products;

iv) It thus has the largest variety of skills and occupations;

ii) The companies which are mostly transnational or multinational or foreign, with an increasing number of Nigerian-owned in the service sector;

2) The number of the companies at any point in time depends on the investment policies of oil/gas producing companies, usually in response to government's own investment in the industry and provision of required cash call in respect of joint-projects. Drilling and other jobs are then subcontracted to companies in the Oil/Gas industry;

3) This means that the contracts are short-term, just as the jobs on offer are time-bound or short-term;

4) The short-term nature of the contracts between oil-producing companies and oil/gas services companies deeply impacts on labour-management relations within the service companies.

Views of members of Management

a) What comes across is the existence of widespread unease over the state of industrial relations in the industry. In spite of this, it was routinely maintained that labour-management relations are generally good because of the absence of major strikes.

b) Management seemed to have two likely reasons for the current state of affairs: a) the legacy of the past, derived largely from accumulated grievances and poor state of relations between representatives of employees and some members of management who have since been redeployed or posted out of the country; b) "increasing militancy of approach" on the part of the unions and workers.

c) Union leaders use their roles as self-serving tools to solve on-the-job and career problems, as some only became active unionists or members of their executive committees as a result of career/personal problems. Otherwise, management feels it has been managing the whole situation fairly well but for the surprising hostile reaction of the unions.

d) Relations with PENGASSAN more stable, and the tendency on the part of NUPENG to make "unrealistic" demands is quite high, rendering relations more conflictual.

e) In general, the unions lack communication skills in the expression and representation of their members' needs and requirements.

f) That union leaders always seek to prevent management addressing the mass of employers/union members on controversial/other issues, thereby affording the former (i.e., union leaders) the opportunity to misrepresent events and disseminate inaccurate information designed to inflame tempers or turn them against company policies.

g) That compensation levels and other fringe benefits or entitlements are most competitive in the economy and wonder why employees do not feel satisfied.

h) Training programmes have been stepped up in the last few years, with employees keener on programmes taking place overseas. Self-improvement is also greatly encouraged.

i) That there is the habit of some union leaders to seek the monetisation of certain benefits, e.g. educational assistance.

Workers and their organisations – their views

a. The unions say the existing climate of industrial relations in the industry is characterised by "low trust relations". Two things have created the low trust relations: a) lack of transparency; and b) lack of integrity on management's side. The lack of transparency and lack of integrity are always displayed by management in dealing with the work force and the unions: hoarding information and statistics; failure to keep 'gentlemen's agreement' on several occasions; and reneging on formal agreements, etc.

b. Management style is largely autocratic and dictatorial, and embarking on half-hearted attempts at dialoguing only after things have gone out of hand. That once production is not affected, management remains slow and lethargic over issues: it is not proactive because of relative indifference.

c. The apparent lack of career path. Workers and unions believe that there are "no standards, no guidelines, and no rules", leading to arbitrariness in placements and promotions and thus favouritism and discrimination.

d. Concerning appraisals, that individual relations are assessed, not competence and performance, and there are always inconsistencies/divergent positions in both staff and manager's appraisal that are ever resolved in a fair and transparent manner. In a worst-case scenario, there was zero scoring in the appraisal exercise when none actually took place for the staff. That the whole process is characterised by bad faith, poor handling of documents, no formal feedback given to those appraised and is a mere ritual conducted to justify management's biases or preferred options rather than a true reflection of the performance and competence of staff concerned.

e. As part consequence of item d) immediately above, sometimes designations/positions do not carry the responsibilities and powers that should go with them, especially between Nigerian and expatriate management staff. In general, promotion is a problem at the lower levels, while most staff in the middle rungs have nowhere to move to not just because of the pyramidal structure of the organisation but also because provisions have not been made.

f. Great disenchantment with the HR Department, viewed largely to be functioning merely as an instrument for implementing the 'hidden agenda' of management.

g. Flowing from item e), that most Nigerians occupying fairly important management positions tend to be ineffective in fostering more cordial labour-management relations because of their seeming preoccupation with protecting their positions and privileges. There is the suggestion that such persons are promoted or picked more for their strong pro-employer orientation.

h. Industrial relations are not taken seriously hence it remains one of the items in the portfolio of the Employee Relations Officer or HR Manager. Or, rather, that *Employee Relations* (focus on the individual employee) and *Community Relations* have been substituted for *Industrial and Labour Relations* and which, perhaps, explains why things are that bad and why management merely *reacts* to developments rather than be *proactive.*

i. Training is not taken seriously for many reasons. One, it has become part of the patronage system – 'a weapon, settlement, bribe or a favour'. Two, there is no 'focused training' because priorities are not known. Three, no effective training in the absence of a career path. And, four, as a result, a good many training programmes scheduled for staff have no bearing to current job functions.

j) The most conflict-prone department is Production. Some of the reasons for this include a) the domination of the Department by expatriates who are often on time-bound and/or contract staff; b) have little regard for communication skills; c) are not particularly concerned with the terms of employment and other human resource issues of local staff.

k) That the record on managing cultural diversity has been poor, damaging and counter-productive, serving to increase tensions, demands, protests as well as leading to lower morale and declining productivity. First, that there are two parallel organisations, one for expatriates and the other for Nigerians and thus both groups have no sense of belonging to and working for the same company. Expatriates have a career and their terms of employment are not only far more attractive, kept secret, but also managed from abroad. Second, that expatriate staffs, despite sometimes inferior skills and qualifications and shortcomings in several other departments, have tended to wield more power and influence than the highest placed Nigerian staff. That jobs are deliberately created for expatriates, who are all always placed in the senior staff category, to get experience in Nigeria although many clearly lack management skills. Third, there is discrimination against Nigerian staff in the access to and use of company facilities, stringent conditions being deliberately imposed to limit such access and use by non-expatriates. Fourth, for the Nigerian staff, recruitment, placement and promotion have been coloured or influenced by ethnic and other parochial consideration. As such, sycophancy and 'godfatherism' are on the increase.

l)   That outsourcing and subcontracting often encourage exploitation of employees, while sometimes creating jurisdictional disputes for the unions.

Challenges offered by oil-bearing communities

We approach some of the challenges posed by host communities from two perspectives having cover other aspects under Community Relations: i) that of the corporate organisation; and ii) of individual employee. In practice, of course, some of the implications for these categories of actors may be difficult to separate, but the classification provides a fairly systematic way of discussing the issues.

i) Corporate organisation

Some businesses have rightly regarded oil-producing or oil-bearing communities, or host communities, especially for the past thirty years, as an aspect of the larger environment that they can no longer ignore nor take for granted. This is particularly so where effluents, emissions, spillages and other pollutants have become subject of considerable disapproving local and international attention.

Recruitment, selection, placement and promotions have become more sensitive issues, host communities routinely demanding positions for "indigenes" or their "sons and daughters". The management of local aspect of such diversity has become compounded in some companies by the relative influx of expatriate personnel which outsourcing through service providers has done little to stem. A by-product of this has been allegations of the adoption of non-objective criteria in matters of recruitment, placement, promotion and, even, choice of staff for cross-postings in those transnational companies that practise it.

There is some evidence of strategic co-operation between law enforcement agencies and management and where such is not properly managed and leads to the adoption of strong-arm tactics (like in Odi and a few other places), we end with a cycle of violence. So, otherwise commendable contributions of companies and other international donors to capacity building of the police and other law enforcement agencies get denounced as "evil alliance".

Individual employee

It could be argued that for the average employee, the host community's reactions have little or no impact on the job or life, except where employees of the company are specific targets of violence, abduction, and other acts considered threatening to their peace and security. Even at that, some would point out, expatriate or well-placed employees are often the victims or likely targets.

Be that as it may, some employees who are "sons and daughters" from the host communities have behaved in a manner to suggest their being entitled to privileges or some positions or rapid promotion or larger representation. A few have sought the intervention of more prominent "son" or "daughter" or traditional authority to achieve such aspirations.

For day-to-day employee relations and in times of conflict the status of being a "son" or "daughter" would tend to lead to ambivalence, depending on company's policy: either being a source of information for and generally in support of management, or swinging to the other extreme of hostility and aggressiveness.

For the reaction of other employees who do not come from the host community, employee relations would likely depend substantially on the importance accorded by management to local employees or indigenes. Where this is given much attention, other employees are likely to feel discriminated against except where such "affirmative action" is restricted to the lower rungs of the hierarchy. In which case, both the host community and "sons" and "daughters" therein are likely to demand more representation at the middle and higher levels of the hierarchy. The larger point here is that where diversity management is not competently handled, and employees as a consequence generally evaluate developments and day-to-day labour management relations through sectional or ethnic prisms, motivation and maintenance of discipline tend to be problematic.

Although outsourcing and use of external contractors as service providers has been on the increase in recent times due to keener competition brought about by globalisation and attendant so-called neo-liberal macroeconomic policies (deregulation, privatisation and liberalisation, etc.), it has been suggested host communities' reactions to businesses, particularly in the oil and gas industry, have further accelerated the process, businesses attempting to wash their hands off recruitment of "non-core" staff. Staff with open-ended employment contracts and those on much shorter-term contracts offered by subcontractors or service providers have equally showed some anxiety over compensation levels, future of the job and career path.

It would also be true to say that purely internal affairs of trade unions, especially power tussles and non-transparent activities, can impact negatively on the union, members and, sometimes, organisational productivity.

The challenges facing union leadership in the oil and gas industry are many and largely derive from the strategic nature of the industry and the fact of subcontracting and outsourcing being the dominant modes for obtaining goods and services. These are then complicated by the relatively tender age of the average employee who is often better educated than before, articulate and skilled, but operate in a labour market characterised by great uncertainty due to short-term contracts oil and gas service companies have with their clients - the oil-producing and marketing companies. This suggests that union membership would tend to fluctuate, in line with the life span of jobs or projects secured by employing companies. A further consequence is that the oil and gas industry has the greatest mix or variety of skills and occupations, thereby posing organisational and collective bargaining challenges to union leadership. Finally, diversity management shall continue to present challenges, with respect to career path, compensation levels, future of the job and composition of the work force in particular.[47]

How about trades unions strategies and tactics?

Typologies of 'role' of unions in Africa are replete, the commonest being 'productionist' as against 'consumptionist'. Along another dimension, using political party-unions relationship as criterion, others are 'integrated' versus 'opposition' or 'independent'." The 'independence' of Nigerian unions as identified along the latter dimension by Robin Cohen[48] needs ˉseveral qualifications. Firstly, top trade union leaders have always belonged to different political parties and with a divided central leadership in the form of numerous central labour organizations, the unions have often been pulled in different directions. Secondly, trade union members, like most other literate and semiliterate Nigerians, have fully participated in sectional politics of the day; some of them assuming prominent positions in erstwhile ethnic or 'tribal' associations."

If at the enterprise level the emphasis of unionism is on better conditions of service, conversion of daily-paid workers into permanent category and a change in racial and national composition of

---

[47] The 'inevitability' of co-operation between antagonistic forces in industry was since pointed out by Trotsky:

There is one common feature in the development, or more correctly, the degeneration of modern trade union organisations in the entire world: it is their drawing closely to and growing together with the state power. The process is equally characteristic of the neutral, the Social-Democratic, the Communist and "anarchist" trade unions. This fact alone shows that the tendency towards "growing together" is intrinsic not in this or that doctrine as such but it derives from social conditions common for all unions.

[48] *Labour and Politics in Nigeria, op. cit.*

managements (which, at any rate is partly what the indigenization decrees are aimed at especially with provisions for 'expatriate quota' and 'local content' respectively), the institutional isolation of trade unions has not been as great as some observers imagine. Most labour leaders, from available evidence, seem fairly nationalistic and tend to accept government's budgets and do subscribe to the whole and quite untenable belief in 'catching up with the developed countries' - and the 'national sacrifices' that go with it. That most of them are galvanized into more intransigent posturing by activities of workers has been proved again and again, activities themselves that are predicated upon issues clearly delineated by respective wages commissions and government policies. What all this amounts to is that if trade unions in socialist-oriented countries in Africa and elsewhere are described as 'integrated', trade unions in capitalist countries, neo-colonial or not, can hardly escape the label of 'collaborationist' - notwithstanding the presence of a very vocal section. That any labour organization can criticize the government and indeed offer alternative set of programmes may be a reflection of prevailing democratic situation and not necessarily an index of independence. That the established channels of communication, including the lobbying of members of parliament, are utilised and deference to constituted authorities still prevail, not to mention a general concern over the declining British or American or Nigerian economic standing, do suggest a degree of interdependence and compatible 'ideologies' that the pluralist ideologues are not tired of pointing out. Having said this, one should also recognize that some workers are dedicated to the establishment of an alternative kind of society; the only problem seems to be the number imbued with such a vision.

Given the less complex nature of the Nigerian economy, the ideological coloration of the trade union movement may not be as problematic as made out to be. Nigeria, for example, has no historical experience of truly revolutionary movements, no radical intellectual activity and cultural expectations have been distorted by the western-educated elite that confusedly associate 'consumerism' and mimicry of European ways with 'modernity' and 'development'. The acceptance of wealth as a success symbol and acquisition of electronic gadgets and other consumer items which has spread across all social classes, workers and trade unionists not excepted, tend to create an environment most unconducive to critical appraisal of the economic set up. We have seen over the years that Nigerian workers, though establishing workers' capacity to organize in protection of their corporate interest, reveal the ultimate ambition of the low-paid worker to be 'self-employment' (an understandable reaction to economic insecurity with preferred occupations as petty trading and some form of 'business' requiring small initial capital outlay) and not the *replacement* of the capitalist system. Radicalism is in this sense related to the readiness to resort to the strike weapon over issues already determined by the various wages commissions. The degree of violence involved may only be inversely related to the intransigence of various managements (including the government as an employer) in meeting officially announced awards and gradings, and not 'threats' to the power-structure.

Like nationalism, 'ethnicism', a factor which cuts across social classes, has been inadequately dealt with by both Marxism and orthodox/ecletic analysis. Both analytical approaches not only view ethnicism as primordial sentiments and historically 'archaic' but also imply that its consequences could be nothing as great as those of inter-class conflict. Along with religious and other community conflicts, ethnic conflict is viewed as irrational, a state that would be overwhelmed by proletarianization and its accompanying class consciousness as mentioned earlier. Liberal political theory pretends that a constituency is populated by persons of similar social needs and thus any chosen representative would be quite effective. Whereas, the supposedly socialist Soviet Union of old took greater care to devise a constitution that not only made movement between each of the internal republics a difficult business but also provided for the representation of all racial and other minority groups. Even if not carried out to the letter in practice, such constitutional provisions do represent a greater sensitivity to racial and other ethnic problems and less dependence on the magic of proletarian consciousness.

And, as noted above, European and North American trade unionism may provide little guidance to Nigerian trade union leaders faced with a multi-ethnic situation. To deprecate 'tribalism' or 'ethnic chauvinism' in the Nigerian labour movement hardly sheds light on the problems accompanying the organizing of a multi-ethnic labour force. To dismiss ethnic consciousness as a hindrance to the emergence of workers' class consciousness may even be a poor conception of social reality and an inadequate grasp of the problems associated with self-identity. If only to misquote Frank Parkin and parody Karl Marx, it seems quite possible for a man to think of himself as an industrial worker in the morning, an Isoko or Efik or Yoruba or Italian-American, Irish-American or Catalan in the afternoon, and a Nigerian or American or Spanish in the evening without any difficulty. In short, that class and ethnic identities can simultaneously be held and activated hardly signifies less proletarianization. It stays likely that a student of the working classes in Northern Ireland (where the Irish are at loggerheads with descendants of English settlers), Belgium (where the Flemings and Walloons are implacably opposed), and the United States of America (where the tendency is for specific racial groups to dominate unionism in certain industries) would think multi-faceted identities more humanlike. The overwhelming numerical dominance of the English over the Scots, Welsh, Irish, Asians and Africans and West Indians in Britain, and near homogeneity of the French, German and Italian populations may have clouded this issue in the realm of unionism.

The point of all this is that there is nothing peculiarly African or Nigerian about a member of the proletarian class displaying some other form of consciousness considered less rational or scientific. The peculiarly European reaction has been, so it seems from historical evidence, to exclusively organize either along racial or religious lines: there never seems to have been any serious attempts on multi-racial or multi-religious basis without the unwritten understanding of the dominance of a particular group or religion. There thus seems to be no sufficient grounds for the widely-held assumption of the 'homogenizing influence of the modern industrial state would be too powerful to allow the survival of traditionalistic and narrower tribal loyalties that flourished under agrarian systems'.' In spite of the long history of industrial work and unionism, recourse has frequently been taken to ethnic-racial and religious sympathies in times of union elections in some European and North American countries. Nigerian unionists have not been remarkably different.

One may, of course, foresee the possibility of the emergence of a less efficient, or even corrupt, labour leader because of blatant exploitation of these sympathies, but the tactics adopted for maintaining or assuming positions of power have not been famous for their technical, ethical or moral purity - not even in proletarian organizations.' But in the Nigerian experience, a significant proportion of the top labour leaders (including Michael Imoudu, Frank Kokori, Adams Oshiomhole) have come from the so-called minority ethnic groups; a fact that suggests considerable success in organizing across ethnic lines and which is also reflected in the careful attention paid to ethnic composition of executives of the various central labour organizations.

Although most observers habitually identify 'political attitudes' of Nigerian workers, it is too easily forgotten that colonial administration and military governments in Nigeria have been authoritarian and that the country has only had a short spells of civilian government as at today. Demographic changes have ensured that few workers have experienced the three phases nor can one assume literacy and political socialization (or consciousness) have enabled most people to become aware of political 'alternatives'. The only measure of continuity is provided by an elite, which still in its formative stages, has been recruiting from all segments of the population - teachers, professionals and intellectuals, businessmen, failures in all walks of life (especially business) and trade unionists.

The relevance of the above can be seen in respect of the ultimate career goals of labour leaders: of the 150 labour leaders interviewed 100 expected to end up in 'business' or 'politics', 50 of who admitted to having 'laid the foundation' (meaning that they had investments and were also involved in clandestine political groupings). Their conception of authority and leadership, it also appeared, was derived from two mutually reinforcing factors: of being the 'early leaders', 'those who fought for independence' (thus quite paternalistic) and the colonial-style (and authoritarian) total control of subordinates which left no room for opposition. These tendencies were reinforced by the then existing Nigerian political parties which made impossible political activities outside their framework. The reference group of labour leaders became their 'counterparts' in politics (who gained power because of being 'early leaders'), a category that was still recruiting and labour leaders were logically qualified candidates. Having been deprived access to the general population by 'politicians', it could be said that most labour leaders regarded the labour movement as their 'constituency', a card up their sleeves with which to command access to political office and to respect from their 'counterparts' in politics. For some, the labour movement was thus simply used as a vehicle for upward mobility as neither labour leaders educational attainments nor the scope and direction of external interests' 'educational activities' appreciably enhanced their statuses. Indeed labour leaders, thanks to external interests and business acumen (in a few cases, use of union funds), acquired cars and paraded around like their 'counterparts' - cars are a status symbol in Nigeria - and tended to supplicate for traditional titles and chieftaincies (again like their 'counterparts') by virtue of the fact of being 'leaders' and of being 'important sons and daughters' of their communities or hometowns.

These tendencies have necessarily affected the affairs of individual trade unions and workers' activities. As previously mentioned, labour leaders sitting on Arbitration and Labour Advisory Boards have, for all these reasons, tended to promote ideas and policies workers have had to reject. But more crucial has been the general adverse effect on organizational strategies. Adrian Peace in his excellent participant observation study of the strikes over 'Adebo' awards in 1970 in the Ikeja industrial estate (suburb of Lagos), has provided the most direct evidence that Nigerian workers have developed a fairly explicit consciousness of their class position *vis-à-vis* others and evolved tactics to deal with their environment." Paul Lubeck in another fascinating study of unorganized workers in three enterprises in Kano has shown the ability of workers to develop strategies and cope with management's tactics while substituting 'class-based loyalties' for 'communal loyalties'. But, the *upper* limits of this consciousness have been set, among other reasons, by the disjunction between central leadership's aims and goals and those of unions and by the lack of opportunity for leaders thrown up by workers at the *plant level* to move into central leadership. These limitations have then been reinforced by the imposed *choice* of issues as set by the relevant wages tribunal or commission or government policy/pronouncement. Simplified almost to the absurd, it is all similar to a common practice in various African communities whereby for a specified period during some festive occasions all *taboos* are, as it were, suspended. On these occasions outrageous and anti-social behaviour takes place - but at the end of the festival everyone behaved as if nothing had happened. In this sense, most workers' protests have been 'enacted' for the commissions and certain policies have clearly set limits and issues in dispute whatever 'threats to the power structure' any observer may have noted on these occasions. From the 'structure of the situation' and from the writer's own experience at Ibadan in respect of 'Adebo' awards, even participants themselves (workers, government officials and management) realized their *temporariness,* with the exception of the Udoji awards which involved many other factors as previously indicated. Such transience has been confirmed by the *inability* of central leadership to tap workers' consciousness and provide it with a coherent and systematic ideological position. Explicit worker class consciousness has thus occurred in *starts* and has not, so far as the observer can judge, brought serious challenges to managerial authority in respect of workload or job content. Same for nationwide strikes between 1999 and 2014 over official increases in pump-prices of refined petroleum products which drew in various segments of society.

Concluding remarks

Mr Vice Chancellor, I should like to end by suggesting the following:
1)   John Dunlop should be told that there are more than three 'social actors' in an industrial relations system as evidenced in our analysis;

2)   That Karl Marx should advise ALL that:
   a) in social and human affairs, the thesis-anti-thesis-synthesis-thesis-anti-thesis-synthesis is likely to continue indefinitely as the processes recommended by him for overthrowing the capitalist system are ideal-typical or logical abstractions without belabouring arguments about changed nature of modern capitalism since his days;

b) only a small fraction of any population would be wage earners or workers and they are not the poorest segment, not the most articulate and influential, not the best organised and not the most violent in methods;

c) by the same token, disenchantment, poverty, and whatever else, including widespread workers protests, may lead to revolutions, and as things are they are not likely to be led and controlled by workers and their organisations. Few Labour Parties are controlled by workers', and not many have enjoyed wide acceptance;

3) all societies will be socially stratified – even in worker-controlled enterprises or organisations, providing some of the bases for alienation, conflict and further contradictions despite reduced inequalities - as reaction to the "Dictatorship of the Proletariat", which is remote for now in Nigeria, should elicit counter-reaction as other dictatorship;

4) emphasize that "I" versus "You", "Us" versus "Them" as bases for decisions and actions are not merely functions of economic and political ideologies or systems; they are also basic socio-psychological processes, as instinctive as a drive to protect one's life and property – and are routinely activated under a variety of circumstances, not just work-related situations rendering problematic an "inevitable" future dominance of Proletarian Consciousness;

5) that social scientists, especially in Africa, should pull back, undertake more critical reflections because the signs are that, with current economic and socio-political developments and incredible advancements in information and communication technologies, the blinkers imposed by long-dominant orthodoxies and concepts have begun to decompose and lift themselves with DE-MODELLING of models and a better understanding of prototypes in their true nakedness;

6)   permit me to crave your indulgence to remind me when next I am in Southern Africa to find out from the Bushmen of Kalahari Desert, what they call themselves;

7)   The institutional transfer thesis, it is here argued, is a myth, an illusion;

8)   It is not a claim to Nigerian (or African or Asian) "exceptionalism", but a claim to *exceptionalism* of ALL individual or country-experiences.

9)   that at the end of the day, from California, New York, London, Paris, Tokyo, Peking, Berlin, Delhi and everywhere else to Lagos, we all are BUSHMEN in the face of incomplete knowledge, production and distribution of goods and services based on private preferences, human passions and perversions, and about the only thing we might practically and theoretically be sure of is economic boom surely being followed by economic depression, what Karl Marx wrote about a long time ago; all else are partly ego-centric and partly-racist modelling and trade in illusions for ideological, political and other self-serving reasons.

References and Select Bibliography

Abercrombie, N, Hill, S. & Turner, B.S., *The Dominant Ideology Thesis*, Allen & Unwin, London, 1980.

Abiodun, A. O., *Restructuring of Trade Unions in Nigeria, 1976-1978*, Salama Press, Jos, 1978

Adeogun, A. A., 'Strikes and the Institutionalization of Labour Protest: the Case of Nigeria', *Seminar on Third World Strikes*, Hague, 1977.

Akpala, A., 'Industrial Relations Policies in Nigeria', *Genieve-Afrique, vol.* 10(1), 1971.

Akpala, A., *Industrial Relations Model for Developing Countries: the Nigerian System,* Fourth Dimensions Press, Enugu, 1982.

Akpala, A., *Managing Industrial Relations in' Nigeria: A Case Study of the Nigerian Coal Industry,* Dept. of Management of Univ: of Nigeria, Nsukka, 1984.

Alavi, H., 'The State in Postcolonial Societies,' *New Left Review, vol.* 74, 1972.

Albrow, M., *Bureaucracy*, Macmillan, London, 1970

Aldridge, A., *Power, authority and restrictive practices*, Blackwell, Oxford, 1976

Allen, V.L., *Militant Unionism*, Merlin, London, 1966

-The Sociology of Industrial Relations, Longman, 1971.

-Social Analysis: a Marxist Critique and Alternative, Longman, London, 1975

Amin, S., *Neocolonialism in West Africa,* Penguin, 1973.

Ananaba, W. *The Trade Union Movement in Nigeria,* Ethiope Publish ing Company, Benin, 1969.

Alavi, H., 'The Post-Colonial State,' *New Left Review*, 1974

Anthony, P.D., *The Ideology of Work*, Tavistock, London, 1977

Arrighi, G. and Saul, John S., Essays on the political economy of Africa, Monthly Review Press, New York, 1973

Bachrach, P. & Baratz, M.S., 'Decisions and Non-decisions,' *American Political Science Review*, 1963, Vol. LVII, pp. 641-51

Baldamus, W., *Efficiency and Effort*, Tavistock, London, 1961

Bain, S. & Clegg, H.A., 'Strategy for Industrial Relations Research in Great Britain,' *British Journal of Industrial Relations*, 1974, Vol. III, No 1.

Banks, J.A., *Marxist Sociology in Action*, Faber & Faber, London, 1970

- *Trade Unionism*, Collier-Macmillan, London, 1974

Baran, P., *The Political Economy of Growth*, Monthly Review Press, New York, 1957

- & Sweezy, P., *Monopoly Capital,* Penguin, Harmondsworth, 1966

Barnard, C.I. , *The Functions of the Executive*, Harvard University Press, 1958.

Bartos, O.J., 'Simple Model of Negotiation,' in Zartman, W. I. (ed.) *The Negotiation Process; theories and applications*, Sage Publications, Beverly Hills & London, 1978

Batstone, E., *Working Order: Workplace Industrial Relations over Two Decades*, Blackwell, Oxford, 1984

- Boraston, I. and Frankel, S., *Shop Stewards in Action: the Organisation of Workplace Conflict and Accommodation*, Blackwell, Oxford, 1977.

- Boraston, I. and Frankel, S., *The Social Organisation of Strikes*, Blackwell, Oxford, 1978

- Ferner, A. and Terry, M., *Consent and Efficiency: Labour Relations and Management Strategy in the State Enterprise*, Blackwell, Oxford, 1984.

Behrend, H., 'The Effort Bargain,' *Industrial and Labour Relations Review*,' Vol. 10, pp. 503-15

Bendix, R., *Work and Authority in Industry*, Univ. of California Press, Berkeley, 1974 (first published in 1956 by Wiley, New York).

Berg, E.J. 'Urban Real Wage and the Nigerian Trade Union Movement 1939-1960: A Comment', *Economic Development and Cultural Change, (EDCC)*, vol. 17(4), 1969.

Berg, E.J. & Butler, J. 'Trade Unions' in J.S. Coleman & C.G. Rosberg, (eds.), *Political Parties and National Integration in Tropical Africa*, Univ. of California Press, Berkeley & Los Angeles, 1964.

Beynon, H. & Blackburn, R. M., *Perceptions of Work*, CUP, Cambridge, 1972

Blackaby, F. (ed.), *De-Industrialisation*, Heinemann, London, 1978

Blake, P.R. & Mouton, J.S., *The managerial grid*, Gulf, Houston, Texas, 1964

Blain, A.N.J. & Gennard, J., 'Industrial Relations Theory: a Critical Review,' *British Journal of Industrial Relations*, 1970, Vol. VII, No 3, pp. 389-392.

Blau, P. M, *The Dynamics of Bureaucracy: a Study of Interpersonal Relations in Two Government Agencies*, University of Chicago Press, Chicago, 1963

- & Scott, W.R., *Formal Organisations*, RKP, London, 1963

Blumberg, P., *Industrial Democracy: The Sociology of Participation*, Constable, 1968.

Bowen, P., *Social Control in Industrial Organisations*, RKP, London, 1976

Bradshaw, A., 'Critical Note: a Critique of Steven Lukes' "Power: a Radical View",' *Sociology*, 1976, Vol. 10 Jan. 121-7

Braverman, H., *Labor and Monopoly Capital: the Degradation of Work in the Twentieth Century*, Monthly Review Press, New York, 1974.

Brown, G., *Sabotage: a Study in Industrial Conflict*, Spokesman, Nottingham, 1977.

Brown, W., 'A consideration of custom and practice,' *British Journal of Industrial Relations,'* 1972, vol. 10, pp. 42-61

- *Piecework Bargaining*, Heinemann, London, 1973

- & Jacques, E., *Glacier Project Papers*, Heinemann, London, 1965
Burawoy, M., 'Toward a Marxist Theory of the Labor Process: Braverman and Beyond,' *Politics and Society*, 1978, Vol. 8, nos. 3-4, 247-312.
- *Manufacturing Consent: Changes in the Labor Process under Monopoly Capitalism*, University of Chicago Press, Chicago, 1979.
- 'The Politics of Production and the Production of Politics: a Comparative Analysis of Piecework Machine Shops in the United States and Hungary,' *Political Power and Social Theory,* 1980, vol. 1, pp. 261-99.
- 'Terrains of Contest: Factory and State under Capitalism and Socialism,' *Socialist Register,* 1981, no. 58,   pp. 83-124.
- *The Politics of Production*, Verso, London, 1985
Burrell, G & Morgan, G., *Sociological Paradigms and Organisational Analysis*, Heinemann, London, 1979
Cameron, D., *My Tanganyika Service and Some Nigeria,* London, 1939.
Cannon, I.C., 'Ideology and occupational community,' *Sociology*, 1967, May, Vol. 15, no. 2
Cardechi, G., 'Reproduction of social classes at the level of production,' *Economy and Society*, 1975, Vol. 4, no. 4, pp. 361-417.
- *On the Economic identification of social classes*, RKP, London, 1977
Certo, S.C., *Principles of Modern Management,'* W., C. Brown Company, Dubuque, Iowa, 1980
Chamberlain, N.W., *Collective Bargaining,* McGraw-Hill, 1951
Chamberlain, N. & Kuhn, J. , *Collective Bargaining,* (2nd edn), McGraw-Hill, 1965
Chelser, M. A. *et al.,* 'Power training: an alternative path to conflict management,' *California Management Review*, 1978, Vol. XXI, no. 2.
Child, J. (ed.), *Man and Organisation*, Allen & Unwin, London, 1973
- *The Business Enterprise in Modern Industrial Society*, Collier-Macmillan, London, 1969.

Clack, G., *Industrial Relations in a British Car Factory*, Allen & Unwin, London, 1973

Clarke, T & Clements, L. (eds.), *Trade Unions Under Capitalism*, Fontana/Collins, Glasgow, 1977

Clawson, D., *Bureaucracy and the labour process: the transformation of US industry 1860-1920*, Monthly Review Press, New York, 1980

Clegg, H. A., *A New Approach to Industrial Democracy*, Basil Blackwell, 1960.

- *System of Industrial Relations in Great Britain*, 1970
- 'Pluralism in industrial relations,' *British Journal of Industrial Relations*, 1975, Vol. 13.
- *Trade Unionism Under Collective Bargaining*, Blackwell, Oxford, 1976

Clegg, S. & Dunkerley, D., *Organisation, Class and Control*, RKP, London, 1980

Cohen, P. S., *Modern Social Theory*, Heinemann, London, 1968

Cohen, R., 'Further Comment on the Kilby/Weeks Debate', *Journal of Developing Areas,* vol. 5 (2), January 1971

Cohen, R., *Labour and Politics in Nigeria,* Heinemann, 1974.

Cole, G.D.H., *British Trade Unionism Today*, Victor Gollanz, London, 1938

Coleman, J.S. *Nigeria: Background to Nationalism,* Univ. of California Press, Berkeley & Los Angeles, 1958

Coleman, J.S. & Rosberg, C.G., *Political Parties and National Integration in Tropical Africa,* Univ. of California Press, Berkeley & Los Angeles, 1964.

Comte, A., *Cours de Philosphie Positive*, IV

Coser, L., *The Social Functions of Conflict*, RKP, London, 1956

Craig, A.W.J., A Framework for the Analysis of Industrial Relations System, in Barrett, E., Rhodes and Beishson, J., (eds.), *Industrial Relations and the Wider Society*, Collier-Macmillan, London, 1975.

Cressey, P and MacInnes, J., 'Voting for Ford', *Capital and Class*, 1980, no. 11, Summer, pp. 5-34

Crompton, R. and Gubbay, J., *Economy and Class Structure*, Macmillan, London, 1977

Crouch, C., *Class Conflict and Industrial Relations Crisis*, Heinemann, London, 1977

-    *The Politics of Industrial Relations*, Fontana, London, 1979.

-   (ed.) *State and Economy in Contemporary Capitalism,* Croom Helm, London, 1979

-   *Trade Unions: the Logic of Collective Action*, Fontana, 1982

Crowder, M., *The Story of Nigeria,* Faber, London, 1966.

Crowder, M.,*West Africa Under Colonial Rule,* Hutchinson, 1968.

Crozier, M., *The Bureaucratic Phenomenon*, Tavistock, London, 1964

Dahl, R. *Preface to Democratic Theory,* Chicago University Press, 1956.

-   -'The Concept of Power,' *Behavioural Science*, 1957, Vol. 2, July.

-   *Who Governs?*, Yale University Press, New Haven, 1961.

-   *Democratic Theory*, 1967.

-*Pluralist Democracy in America*, Mcnally, Chicago, 1967

Dahrendorf, R. *Class and Class Conflict in Industrial Society,* Routledge & Kegan Paul, London, 1959.

Dalton, M., *Men Who Manage*, Wiley, New York, 1959

Daniel, W.W. & McIntosh, N., *The Right to Manage*, MacDonald/PEP, London, 1972

Dare, L.O. 'Nigerian Military Governments and the Quest for Legitimacy', *Nigerian Journal of Economic and Social Studies,* vol. 17(2), 1975.

Davies, I. 'The Politics of the TUC's Colonial Policy', *Political Quarterly,* vol. 35(1), 1958.

—   *African Trade Unions*, Penguin, Hammondsworth, 1966.

Drucker, P., *The Practice of Management*, Harper & Row, New York, 1954

Drucker, P., *People and Performance*, William Heinemann, London, 1977.

Dubin, R., 'Power and union-management relations,' *Administrative Science Quarterly*, 1957, vol. 2, pp. 66-81.

-   'A theory of conflict and power in union-management relations,' *Industrial and Labour Relations Review*, 1960, vol. 13, no. 4.

-Human Relations in Administration, 2nd Edn., Prentice-Hall, Englewood Cliffs, 1961

Dudley, B.J. 'Violence in Nigerian Politics', *Transition,* vol. 5, 1965.

— 'Federalism and the Balance of Political Power in Nigeria', *Journal of Commonwealth Political Studies,* vol. 4, 1966.

— *Parties and Politics in Northern Nigeria,* Frank Cass, London, 1968.

— *Instability and Political Order: Politics and Crisis in Nigeria,* University of Ibadan Press, Ibadan, 1973.

Dunkerley, D. and Salaman, G. (eds.), *The International Yearbook of Organisation Studies*, RKP, London, 1980

Dunlop, J.T. *Industrial Relations System,* Southern Illinois Univ. Press, Carbonsdale & Edwardsville, 1958.

Edwards, R.C., 'The social relations of production in the firm and labour market structure,' *Politics and Society*, 1975, vol. 4.

- *et al., Labour Market Segmentation*, D.C. Heath, Lexington, Mass., 1975

-   *Contested Terrain: the Transformation of the Workplace in the Twentieth Century*, Heinemann, London, 1979.

Ekundare, R.O. *An Economic History of Nigeria,* 1860-1960, Methuen, London, 1973.

— 'Salary and Wages Reviews Since 1946', *Quarterly Journal of Administration,* Ife, Oct. 1971-1972 July.

Eldridge, J.E.T., *Industrial disputes: essays in the sociology of industrial relations*, RKP, London, 1968

Elger, A., 'Valorization and deskilling: a critique of Braverman,' *Capital and Class*, 1979, no. 7. Spring.

- & Schwarz, B., 'Monopoly capitalism and the impact of Taylorism: notes on Lenin, Gramsci, Braverman and Shon-Rethel,' in Nichols, T. (ed.) *Capital and Labour*, Fontana, London, 1980

Elliot, D. & Elliot, R., *The Control of Technology*, Wykeham, London, 1976

Elliot, J., *Conflict or Co-operation? The Growth of Industrial Democracy*, Kogan Page, London, 1978

Emiola, A. *Nigerian Labour Law*, Univ. of Ibadan Press, 1980.

Etzioni, E., *Complex Organisations*: *A Sociological Reader*, Holt & Rinehart, London, 1966

Ezera, K. *Constitutional Developments in Nigeria*, Cambridge University Press, 1960.

Falola, T. & Ihonvbere, J. *The Rise and Fall of Nigeria's Second Republic*, Zed Press, London, 1985.

Fanon, F. *The Wretched of the Earth*, Penguin, Harmondsworth, 1967.

Fashoyin, T. *Industrial Relations in Nigeria*, Longman, 1980.

Ferris, P., *The New Militants :Crisis in the Trade Unions*, Penguin, Harmondsworth, 1971

Fidler, J., *The British Business Elite: its attitudes to class, status, and power*, Routledge & Kegan Paul, London, 1981

Flanders, A. & Clegg, H., *The System of Industrial Relations in Great Britain*, 1954

Flanders, A., *Industrial Relations: What is wrong with the System? An Essay on its Theory and Future*, Faber, London, 1965

- 'Collective Bargaining: A Theoretical Analysis,' *British Journal of Industrial Relations*, March 1968.

- (ed.) *Collective Bargaining: Selected Readings*, Penguin, Harmondsworth, 1969

- *Management and Unions*, Faber, 1970.

-The Tradition of Voluntarism,' *British Journal of Industrial Relations*, 1974 November.

Fox, A. *Industrial Sociology and Industrial Relations,* HMSO, London, 1966.

-*A Sociology of Industry,* Collier-Macmillan, London, 1971.

— 'Industrial Relations: A Social Critique of Pluralist Ideology' in J. Child (ed.), *Man and Organisation,* George Allen 8; Unwin, London, 1973.

— *Man Mismanagement,* Hutchinson, London, 1974 (2nd edn, 1985)

— *Beyond Contract,* Faber, London, 1974

-'A note on industrial relations pluralism,' *Sociology,* 1979, January.

Frank, A.G. *Capitalist Underdevelopment in Latin America,* Monthly Review Press, New York, 1969.

Freund, B. *Capital and Labour in Nigerian Tin Mines,* Univ. of Ibadan Press, Ibadan, 1981

Friedman, A.L., *Industry and Labour: class struggle at work and Monopoly Capitalism,* Macmillan, London, 1977.

- 'Responsible Autonomy versus Direct Control over the Labour Process,' *Capital and Class,* 1977, Spring.

Friedman, H. & Meredeen, S., *The Dynamics of Industrial Conflict: lessons from Ford,* Croom Helm, London, 1980

Frost, J. F. *et al.,* *Organizational Reality,* Goodyear Publ. Co. Inc., Santa Monica, 1978

Galenson, W. *Labor in Developing Countries,* Univ. of California Press, Berkeley & Los Angeles, 1963.

Geary, W.N.M. *Nigeria Under Colonial Rule,* Frank Cass, London, 1965.

Giddens, A., 'Power in the recent writings of Talcott Parsons,' *Sociology,* 1968, Vol. 113, pp. 257-72

- *Capitalism and Modern Social Theory,* Cambridge Univ. Press, 1971

& Stanworth, P. (eds), *Elites and Power in British Society,* Cambridge Univ. Press, 1974.

Gintis, H., 'The nature of labour exchange and the theory of capitalist production,' *Review of Radical Political Economics,'* 1976, Vol. 8, no. 2

Goldthorpe, J. & Lockwood, D., Bechhofer, R., & Platt, J., *The Affluent Workers: Industrial Attitudes and Behaviour,* Cambridge University Press, 1968

Goodman, J.B.F. and Whittingham, T.G., *Shop Stewards in British Industry*, McGraw-Hill, London, 1969

Goodman, J.F.B. *et al.*, 'Rules in Industrial Relations Theory: a Discussion,' *Industrial Relations Journal*, 1975, Vol. 16, pp. 14-30

Goodman, J.F.B. *et al., Rule-making and Industrial Peace*, Croom Helm, London, 1977

Gorz, A., *The division of labour: the labour process and class struggle in modern capitalism*, Harvester Press, Hassocks, Sussex, 1976.

Goulbourne, H. (ed.), *Politics and State in the Third World, Macmillan,* London, 1979.

Gouldner, A.W., *Wildcat Strike*, Free Press, New York, 1965

      - *The Coming Crisis of Western Sociology*, Heinemann, London, 1971.

      - *The Dialectic of Ideology and Technology,* Macmillan, London, 1976

Gunder-Frank, A., *Capitalist Underdevelopment in Latin America,* Monthly Review Press, New York, 1969

Gutkind, P.C.W. & Wallerstein, I. (eds.), *The Political Economy of Contemporary Africa,* Sage, Beverley Hills & London, 1976.

Gutkind, P.C.W. & Waterman, P. (eds.), *African Social Studies: A Radical Reader,* Heinemann, London, 1977.

Gutkind, P.C.W., Cohen, R., Copans, J. *(eds.), African Labor History,* Sage, Beverly Hills & London, 1978.

Harbison, F.H. & Myers, C.A. (eds.), *Management in the Industrial World*, McGraw-Hill, New York, 1959.

Hill, S.,'Norms, groups and power: the sociology of workplace industrial relations,' *British Journal of Industrial Relations*, 1974, Vol. 12, July, 213-35

      - *Competition and control at work*, Heinemann, London, 1981

Hodgkin, T. *Nationalism in Colonial Africa,* Frederick Muller, 1956.

Hodgkin, T., *African Political Parties,* Penguin, 1961.

Hoogvelt, A. Indigenization and Foreign Capital: Industrialisation in Nigeria,' *Review of African Political Economy, 14,* January—April, 1979.

Hopkins, A.G. The Lagos Strike of 1897: an Exploration in Nigerian Labour History', *Past & Present,* vol. 35, 1966.

— *An Economic History of West Africa,* Longman, 1973.

Hoxie, R., *Trade Unionism in the United States,* Appleton, N. Y., 1917.

Hunnius, G., Garson, G.D. & Case, J. (eds.), *Workers' Control: a reader on labour and social change,* Random House, New York, 1973.

Hyman, R., *The Workers' Union,* Clarendon Press, 1971.

Hyman, R. *Industrial Relations: A Marxist Introduction, Macmillan,* London, 1975.

Ikime, 0. (ed.), *Groundwork of Nigerian History,* Heinemann, Ibadan, 1980.

Johnston, G., *The International Labour Organisation,* Europa Publications, Geneva, 1970

Katz, D. & Khan, R. L., *The Social Psychology of Organisations,* Wiley, NY, 1978 edn

Kilby, P. 'Industrial Relations and Wage Determination: Failure of the Anglo-Saxon Model', *Journal of Developing Areas (JDA).,* vol. 1(14), July 1967.

— 'A Reply to John F. Weeks' Comment', *JDA,* vol. 3(1), October 1968.
- 'Further Comment on the Kilby/Weeks Debate: Final Observations', *JDA,* vol. 5(2), January 1971.

— *Industrialization in an Open Economy: Nigeria 1944-1966,* Cambridge University Press, 1969

Kirk-Green, A. *Crisis and Conflict in Nigeria: Documentary Source-book,* vols. 1&2, OUP, London, 1971.

Kornhauser, A., Dubin, R., & Ross, A. (eds.), *Industrial conflict,* Mc-Graw-Hill, New York, 1954.

Korpi, W. and Shalev, M., 'Strikes, industrial relations and class conflict in capitalist society,' *British Journal of Sociology*, 1979, vol 30, June, pp. 164-87

Knowles, K.,G.J.C., *Strikes: a study in industrial conflict*, Blackwell, Oxford, 1954

Kuhn, J.W., *Bargaining in Grievance Settlement*, Columbia University Press, New York, 1961.

Lammers, C.J., 'Power and participation in decision-making in formal organisations,' *American Journal of Sociology*, 1967, Vol. 73, No. 2

Laski, H., *Trade Unions in the New Society*, Allen & Unwin, London, 1950

Lawrence, P.R. & Lorsch, J.W., *Organisation and Environment: managing differentiation and integration*, Harvard University Press, 1967

Leavitt, *Managerial Psychology*, Univ. of Chicago Press, 1958

Lenin, V.I., *What is to be done?*, Progress Publishers, Moscow

Lipset, S.M. & Bendix, R., *Social Mobility in Industrial Society*, University of California Press, 1959

Little, K. *West African Urbanization: A Study in Voluntary Associations in Social Change,* Cambridge University Press, 1965.

Littler, C. and Salaman, G., Bravermania and beyond: recent theories of the labour process,' *Sociology*, 1982, Vol. 16, no. 2

Lloyd, P.C. (ed.). *The New Elites .of Tropical Africa,* OUP for the International African Institute, London, 1966.

— *Africa in Social Change,* Penguin, 1971.

Lockwood, D., 'Sources of variation in working class images of society,' *Sociological Review*, 1966, Vol. 14, November.

Lozovsky, *The Russian Trade Unions and the NEP*, Paris, p. 10; cited in the 1960 ILO Report on USSR.

Lugard, F.D. *Political Memoranda,* Lagos, 1918. *Report on the Amalgamation of Northern and Southern Nigeria and Administration, 1912-1919,* Cmd. 468, HMSO, London, 1920.

Lupton, T., *On the shopfloor*, Pergamon Press, Oxford, 1973.

Lynd, G.E. (pseud.), *The Politics of African Unionism,* Praeger, New York, 1968.

Maccoby, B., *The Gamesman: the New Corporate Leaders,* Simon & Schuster, New York, 1977.

Mackintosh, J.P. *et al. Nigerian Government and Politics,* Allen & Unwin, 1966.

Malinowski, B., *Argonauts of the Western Pacific,* RKP, 1922
- *A Scientific Theory of Culture,* University of North Carolina Press, 1944

Mandel, E., 'Workers' control and workers' councils,' *International,* 1973, Vol. 2, pp. 1-17

Mann, M., *Consciousness and Action among the Western Working Class,* Macmillan, London, 1973

Mant, A., *The Rise and Fall of the British Manager,* Macmillan, London, 1977.

March, J.G. & Simon, H.A., *Organisations,* Wiley, New York, 1958.

Marcuse, H., *One Dimensional Man: the Ideology of Industrial Society,* Sphere Books, London, 1968.

Margerison, C.J., 'What do we mean by Industrial Relations? A Behavioural science approach,' *British Journal of Industrial Relations,* 1969, Vol. II.

Marsh, A. I., *Concise Encyclopaedia of Industrial Relations,* Gower, 1971

Martin, R., *The Sociology of Power,* RKP, London, 1977

Marx, K., *Capital, Vol. I*
- & Engels, F., *Selected Works, Vol. II,* Moscow, 1970

Melson, R. 'Nigerian Politics and the General Strike of 1964', in Rotberg, R.I. & Mazrui, A. A. (eds.), *Protest and Power in Black Africa,* OUP, New York, 1970.
-The Political Dilemmas of the Nigerian Labor Movement', in U.G. Damachi, & D.H. Seibel, (eds.), -*Social Change and Economic Development in Nigeria,* Praeger, New York, 1973.

Merton, R.K., *Social theory and social structure,* Free Press, 1949

Miliband, R., *the State in Capitalist Society,* Quartet, 1969.

Millen, B. H., *The Political Role of Labor in Developing Countries*, The Brookings Institution, Washington, 1963.

Mintzberg, H., *The Nature of Managerial Work*, Harper & Row, New York, 1973.

Mittleman, J.H.(ed.), *Globalization: critical reflections*, Lynne Rienner, Boulder/London, 1977

Mouzelis, N.P., *Organisation and Bureaucracy*, RKP, London, 1967

Mulvey, *Economic Survey of Trade Unions*, Martin Robertson, London, 1978

Murphy, J.T., *The Workers' Committee*, Pluto Press, London, 1972

Nichols, T., *Ownership, control and ideology*, Allen & Unwin, London, 1969.

- 'Labour and Monopoly Capital,' *Sociological Review*, 1977, pp. 192-4.

- (ed.) *Capital and Labour*, Fontana, London, 1980.

- & Armstrong, P., *Workers Divided*, Fontana, London, 1976.

- & Beynon, H., *Living in Capitalism: Class relations and the modern factory*, RKP, London, 1977

Nicholson, I.F. *The Administration of Nigeria 1900-1960: Men, Methods, and Myths,* Clarendon Press, Oxford, 1969.

Nkrumah, K. *Neo-colonialism: The Last State of Imperialism,* Nelson, 1956.

Offe, C., *Industry and Inequality: the achievement principle in work and social status*, Edward Arnold, London, 1976.

Okonjo, I.M. *British Administration in Nigeria: A Nigerian View,* Nok Publishers, New York, 1974.

Osoba, A.M. (ed.), *Productivity in Nigeria*, NISER, 1980

Osoba, O. 'The Nigerian Power Elite, 1952-1965', in P.C.W. Gutkind, & P. Waterman (eds.), *African Social Studies: A Radical Reader,* Heinemann, London, 1977.

Otobo, D. 'The Nigerian General Strike of 1981,' *Review of African Political Economy,* vol. 22, 1981.

Otobo, D. 'The Political Clash in the Aftermath of the 1981 Nigerian General Strike,' *Review of African Political Economy,* vol. 25, 1982.

Otobo, D. 'Strikes in Nigeria: Some Considerations,' *Nigerian Journal of Economic and Social Studies,* Nov. 1983.

Otobo, D. 'Bureaucratic Elites and Public Sector Wage Bargaining in Nigeria,' *Journal of Modern African Studies,* vol. 24(1), 1986

Otobo, D., *Foreign Interests and Nigerian Trade Unions,* Heinemann, Ibadan, 1986.

Otobo, D., *State and Industrial Relations in Nigeria,* Malthouse Press, Oxford, 1986.

Otobo, D. & Omole, M.(eds.), *Readings in Industrial Relations in Nigeria,* Malthouse Press, Oxford, 1987

Otobo, D., *The Role of Trade Unions in Nigerian Industrial Relations,* Malthouse Press, 1987

Otobo, D., *Further Readings in Nigerian Industrial Relations,* Malthouse, Lagos, 1989

Otobo, D., *Labour Relations in Nigeria,* Malthouse, Lagos, 1993

Otobo, D., *Trade Union Movement in Nigeria: Yesterday, Today and Tomorrow,* Kolagbodi Memorial Foundation, Malthouse, Lagos, 1996

Otobo, D., *Industrial Relations: Theory and Controversies,* Malthouse, Lagos, 2003

Otobo, D., *Essentials of Labour Relations in Nigeria Vol. 1,* Malthouse, Lagos, 2017

Otobo, D., *Essentials of Labour Relations in Nigeria Vol. 2,* Malthouse, Lagos, 2017

Otobo, D., *Essentials of Labour Relations in Nigeria Vol. 3,* Malthouse, Lagos, 2017

Otobo, D., *Reforms and Nigerian Labour and Employment Relations ,* Malthouse, Lagos, 2017

Panter-Brick, K. (ed.) *Nigerian Politics and Military Rule: Prelude to Civil War*, Anthlone Press, London, 1970.

Parkin, F., *Class Inequality and Political Order*, Paladin, London, 1972

Parsons, T., *The Structure of Social Action*, Free Press, Illinois, 1949
- *The Social System*, Free Press, Illinois, 1951
- *Essays in Sociological Theory*, Free Press, Illinois, 1951
- *Economy and Society*, RKP, London, 1959

Peace, A. 'Industrial Protest in Ikeja', in de E. Kadt & G.P. Williams (eds.) *Sociology and Development*, Tavistock, London, 1974.

— *Choice, Class and Conflict: A Study of Southern Nigerian Factory Workers*, Harvester, Brighton, 1979.

Perham, (ed.) *Mining, Commerce and Finance in Nigeria*, Faber & Faber, London, 1948.

Perlman, S., *A Theory of the Labour Movement*, Kelley, New York, 1949 (first published in 1928).

Perrow, C., *Complex Organisations: a critical essay*, Scott, Foresman & Co., 1979

Pettigrew, A., *The politics of organisational decision-making*, Tavistock, London, 1973.

Pollard, S., *The genesis of modern management*, Edward Arnold, London, 1965

Poole, M.P., *Workers' participation in industry*, RKP, London, 1975 (rev. edn in 1978).
- *Theories of Trade Unionism*, RKP, London, Boston and Henley, 1980
- *Industrial Relations: origins and patterns of national diversity*, Routledge & Kegan Paul, London, Boston and Henley, 1986

Post, K.W.J. *The Nigerian Federal Election of 1959: Politics and Administration in a Developing Political System*, OUP for NISER, 1963.

Post, K.W.J. & Vickers, M., *Conflict and Control in an Independent African State: Nigeria 1960-1965*, Heinemann, 1973

Post, K.W.J. & Jemkin, G.D., *The Price of Liberty: Personality and Politics in Colonial Nigeria,* Cambridge University Press, 1973.

Proehi, P. O. *Foreign Enterprise in Nigeria,* University of N. Caroline & OUP, Chapel Hill, London & Ibadan, 1965.

Radcliffe-Brown, A. R., *Structure and Function in Primitive Society,* Cohen & West, London, 1952

Roberts, B.C., *Trade Unions in a Free Society,* Institute of Economic Affairs, London, 1959 .

Roberts, B.C., *Labour in the Tropical Territories of the Commonwealth,* Bell, London, 1964.
-*Trade Union Government and Administration in Britain,* Bell, London, 1965.

Roper, R.I., *Labour Problems in West Africa,* Penguin, 1958.

Rose, M., *Industrial Behaviour,* Pelican, 1985

Salaman, G. & Thompson, K., *Control and Ideology in Organisations,* Open University, Milton Keynes, 1980

Salaman, G., *Work Organisations: Resistance & Control,* Longman, 1979.

Sandbrook, R. & Cohen, R. (eds.), *The Development of An African Working Class,* Longman, London, 1975.

Sayles, L.R., *Managerial Behaviour: administration in complex organizations,* McGraw-Hill, New York, 1964.

Schuchman, A., *Co-determination: Labor's Middle Way in Germany,* Public Affairs Press, Washington, 1957.

Shorter, E. & Tilly, C., *Strikes in France: 1830-1968,* Cambridge University Press, 1974

Sklar, R. *Nigerian Political Parties,* Princeton Univ. Press, 1963.

Slichter, S.H., Healy, J.L. and Livernash, E.R., *The impact of collective bargaining on management,* The Brookings Institute, Washington D.C., 1960

Sofer, C., *Organisations in Theory and Practice,* Heinemann, London, 1972

Sofola, K. *Report of the Commission of Inquiry into the Retail and Ancillary Trades in the Federal Territory of Lagos, Government Printer,* Lagos, 1957.

Sohn-Rethel, A., *Intellectual and Manual Labour: a critique of Epistemology,* Macmillan, London, 1978

Storey, J., *Managerial Prerogative and the Question of Control,* RKP, London, 1983

Strauss, G., 'The shifting power balance in the plant,' *Industrial Relations,* 1962, Vol. 1, May, pp. 65-96

Sydney & Beatrice Webb, *Industrial Democracy,* Longmans, 1897
  - *History of Trade Unions,* 2nd Edn, Longmans, 1920

Tamuno, T.N., *The Evolution of the Nigerian State,* Longman, 1976.

Tannenbaum, A. S., 'Unions', in March, J. G. (ed.), Handbook of Organizations, Rand McNally, 1965.
  - *Control in Organisations,* Mc-Graw-Hill, New York, 1968

Taylor, F.W., *Principles of Scientific Management,* Harper, New York, 1911

Thomas, K.W., Introduction: symposium on conflict in organisations,' *California Management Review,* 1978, Vol. XXI, No. 2.

Thompson, E.P., *The making of the English Working Class,* Penguin, Harmondsworth, 1968

Thurley, K. & Wirdenius, H., *Supervision: a Reappraisal,* Heinemann, London, 1973
  - & Wood, S., *Industrial Relations and management strategy,* Cambridge University Press, 1983

Tokunboh, M. A., *Labour Movement in Nigeria,* Lantern Books, 1985

Toyo, E. *The Working Class and the Nigerian Crisis,* Sketch Publishing Corporation, Ibadan, 1967.

Turner, H.A., *Trade Union Growth, Structure and Policy,* Allen & Unwin, 1962

Turner, T. 'Multinational Companies and Instability of the Nigerian State', *Review of African Political Economy,* vol. 5, 1976.

Ubeku, A.K. *Industrial Relations in Developing Countries: The Case of Nigeria*, Macmillan, London & Basingstoke, 1983.

Walton, R. E. & McKersie, R., A Behavioural Theory of Labour Negotiations, McGraw-Hill, New York, 1965

Warren, W.M. 'Urban Real Wages and the Nigerian Trade Union Movement, 1939-1960', *Economic Development and Cultural Change*, vol. 15(1), October 1966.

— 'Urban Real Wages and the Nigerian Trade Union lovement, 1939-1960: A Rejoinder', *Economic Development and Cultural Change*, vol. 17(4), 1969.

Webb, S. & B, *Industrial Democracy*, Longmans, 1897.

- *History of Trade Unionism*, Longmans, Green & Co., 1911

Weber, M., *The Theory of Social and Economic Organisation*, Free Press, 1964 (first published in 1925).

Weeks, J. 'A Comment on P. Kilby: Industrial Relations and Wage Determination', *Journal of Developing Areas*, vol. 3(1), 1968.

— 'Further Comment on the Kilby/Weeks Debate: An Empirical Rejoinder', *Journal of Developing Areas*, vol. 5(2), Jan. 1971.

— 'The Impact of Economic Conditions and Institutional Forces on Urban Wages in Nigeria', *Nigerian Journal of Economic and Social Studies, vol.* 13(3), Nov. 1971.

Westergaard, J., 'The rediscovery of the cash nexus,' in Miliband, R. (ed.) *The Socialist Register*, Merlin, London, 1970.

- & Resler, H., *Class in a capitalist society*, Penguin, Harmondsworth, 1975

Williams, G. (ed.). *Nigeria: Economy and Society,* Rex Collins, London, 1976.

— *State and Society in Nigeria*, Afrografika, 1980.

Williams, R., *Politics and Technology*, Macmillan, London, 1971.

Willis, P., *Learning to labour*, Saxon House, Farnborough, 1977

Windmuller, J.P. 'External Influences on Labor Organizations in Underdeveloped Countries', *Industrial and Labor Relations Review*, vol. 16, July 1963.

Wood *et al.*, 'Industrial Relations System Concept as a Basis for Theory in Industrial Relations,' *British Journal of Industrial Relations*, 1975, Vol. 13, No. 3, pp. 291-307

Wood, S. (ed.), *The degradation of work*, Hutchinson, London, 1982
  - & Elliot, R., 'A critical evaluation of Fox's radicalisation of industrial relations theory,' *Sociology*, 1977, Vol. 11, Jan. pp. 105-25

Woodward, J., *Industrial Organisation: Theory and Practice*, Oxford University Press, 1965.
  - *Industrial Organisation: Behaviour and control*, Oxford University Press, 1970.

Wrong, D.H., 'Some Problems in defining social problem,' *American Journal of Sociology*, 1968, Vol. 73, pp. 673-81

Yesufu, T.M. *An Introduction to Industrial Relations in Nigeria*, OUP for NISER, 1962.
  — *The Dynamics of Industrial Relations: The Nigerian Experience*, University Press Limited, Ibadan, 1984.

Zeitlin, M., Corporate ownership and control: the large corporation and the capitalist class,' *American Journal of Sociology*, 1974, vol. 79, no. 5.

Zey-Ferrell, M. & Aiken, M., *Complex Organisations: Critical Perspectives*, Scott, Foresman & Co., 1981.

Printed in the United States
By Bookmasters